CALL A
BUSINESS
ANGEL

Practical Funding and Commercial Advice
for Start-Ups, SMEs and Innovators

DR EILEEN DOYLE

First published in 2018 by Major Street Publishing Pty Ltd
PO Box 106, Highett, Vic. 3190
E info@majorstreet.com.au
W majorstreet.com.au
M +61 421 707 983

Ordering information

Quantity sales. Special discounts are available on quantity purchases by corporations, associations and others. For details, contact Lesley Williams using the contact details above.

Individual sales. Major Street publications are available through most bookstores. They can also be ordered directly from Major Street's online bookstore at www.majorstreet.com.au.

Orders for university textbook/course adoption use. For orders of this nature, please contact Lesley Williams using the contact details above.

NATIONAL
LIBRARY
OF AUSTRALIA

A catalogue record for this book is available from the National Library of Australia

ISBN: 978-0-6482941-5-3

Internal design by Production Works
Cover design by Simone Geary
Printed in Australia by McPherson's Printing

10 9 8 7 6 5 4 3 2 1

PRAISE FOR EILEEN DOYLE AND
CALL A BUSINESS ANGEL

Dr Eileen Doyle is one of CSIRO's longest-serving board members – appointed for a decade from 15 February 2006 to 14 February 2016. During this time, Eileen served as Acting Chair, Deputy Chair and Chair of various board committees. Significantly, Eileen played a pivotal role in securing returns to Australian science from CSIRO's Wireless Local Area Network (WLAN) patent, the foundation of today's WiFi and recognised as broadly as by the British Museum's international exhibition, "History of the World in 100 Objects".

The foresight, courage and risk taking of the CSIRO board during Eileen's tenure resulted in significant returns that Australian science benefits from today. These include royalties from WLAN contributing to the creation of the $200m CSIRO Innovation Fund, managed by Main Sequence Ventures, which continues the journey to turn Australian invention into innovation for all our benefit. Eileen's common-sense approach to complex business issues helped us transform a 100-year-old hierarchical organisation into today's simplified, market-facing, customer-centric CSIRO. Our teams are aligned with great Australian industries and driven by a common purpose – to solve Australia's greatest challenges with science.

I thank Eileen for her commitment and expertise in preparing this significant and timely publication and commend it to you.

Dr Larry Marshall, 2018, CSIRO CEO

ABOUT THE AUTHOR

Dr Eileen Doyle has had an extensive career working in large corporations, spanning more than three decades. She has a PhD in Mathematics and Statistics and started her career in a technical role in industry, but she quickly moved to management. In 1993, she was Australia's first Fulbright Scholar in Business Management and she completed an International General Management Program at Columbia University in New York and worked for Paine Webber Investment Bank.

Eileen had an executive career in the steel, building materials, infrastructure and logistics industries and she is now a professional company director. She is a Fellow of the Australian Institute of Company Directors and a member of its National Governance Committee. She is also a Fellow of the Academy of Technological Sciences and Engineering. Eileen was Chairman of Port Waratah Coal Services and Deputy Chairman of CSIRO. Her present roles include Director, Oil Search Ltd, Boral Ltd, GPT Group and The Hunter Angels Trust.

Eileen has also had a long history as a business angel, working with inventors and small businesses to introduce and grow their products. She is a Foundation Fellow of the Australian Association of Angel Investors. She has combined her knowledge and discipline from large corporations with her experience with start-ups to write *Call a Business Angel*. You can visit Eileen's website: www.callabusinessangel.com.

FOREWORD

Eileen has brought her long experience on Boards and as an angel investor to deliver a conversational companion to building your business to commercialise invention. She has collected widely accepted business practices and tools into packaged toolkits and template examples that are complemented by real-world war stories from founders.

You don't need an MBA or hours of study to benefit from Eileen's shared knowledge, just the tenacity to give it a go, which is one of her core messages – persistence and discipline are essential keys to success.

Angel investors are a vital contributor to the success of innovation and Eileen has demonstrated why angel investors are essential to the future success of Australia.

Jordan Green
Founder/President – Melbourne Angels
Founder/Chairman Emeritus – Australian Association of Angel Investors
Trustee – Angel Resource Institute (USA)
Chairman – Asian Business Angel Forum

CONTENTS

Contents

PREFACE

I have written *Call a Business Angel* to give readers a perspective on commercialising a business venture from the viewpoint of an experienced angel investor. In this book, I discuss the innovation ecosystem and where angel investing fits in. I describe how investors think and evaluate ideas and how you can pitch your idea to them. I explore the practical aspects of business management – where most great ideas are lost.

Drawing on my decades of experience as a business angel and an executive and non-executive director across a range of industries, I share with readers the disciplined approach larger businesses take when considering where to invest. I also share some useful toolkits I've developed for small to medium businesses to help commercialise their ideas.

This book is designed to complement the great innovation and free thinking that exists in small, growing companies by providing useful advice and tools that give them a much greater chance of being successful.

Many entrepreneurs and small businesses fail not because of a poor idea but because of poor analysis and execution.

Too many companies and their managers have either forgotten or never knew about the quality basics of analysing ideas and how they contribute to sustained business success.

Call a Business Angel explains the key elements of business evaluation and performance management. It also provides a framework to understand where these elements fit, along with enough detail to give a good understanding of a range of toolkits. The reader can use each of the chapters of this book as a checklist to see whether their business idea can transform into a successful enterprise.

All the techniques mentioned here can be applied to any business venture. The level of detail applicable to your business will depend on its size and complexity, but the underlying principles are valid for even very small businesses. I have tried to give examples in each of the chapters but please use your own examples to see how the tools work.

This book gives you some practical frameworks and tools to help you go from idea generation and pitch right through to sustainable commercialisation.

At the end of a number of the chapters you will find a case study. The case studies come from different industries and businesses at varying stages in their enterprise development. I have had personal involvement with all these companies and it has been a pleasure to be involved in their deliberations, struggles and success.

The case studies are preceded by an introduction from me and then they are written in the words of the founders or key executive. I hope you find them interesting and identify with their stories.

Call a Business Angel is intended to inspire you on your journey from idea creation and pitch to sustainable commercialisation. I believe this book can be a valuable companion on your journey, giving you a balanced amount of inspiration and useful tools and frameworks.

Eileen

*To all the entrepreneurs I have helped
and am yet to help*

CHAPTER ONE
FROM INVENTION TO INNOVATION

Everyone has their own definitions of the two words 'invention' and 'innovation'. My definitions are vital to your understanding of the discussion in this book, and they are:

► **Invention** is the creation of better or more effective products, services, processes, technologies or ideas.

► **Innovation** is the acceptance of that invention by the market, i.e. the invention creates value for which customers will pay.

The innovation ecosystem

Moving inventions through to the commercial benefit of becoming an innovation requires a whole community of contributors.

Some very large corporations can contain that community of contributors within the one organisation and continue to grow their business through continual innovation. They have a contained innovation ecosystem and it can be very effective. These contained ecosystems are well worth studying, but they only explain some of the innovation spectrum.

Most innovation ecosystems go across many contributors to help commercialise ideas or inventions. Figure 1.1 overleaf gives a notional overview of the categories of players and their contributions to innovation success.

Figure 1.1 – The Innovation Ecosystem

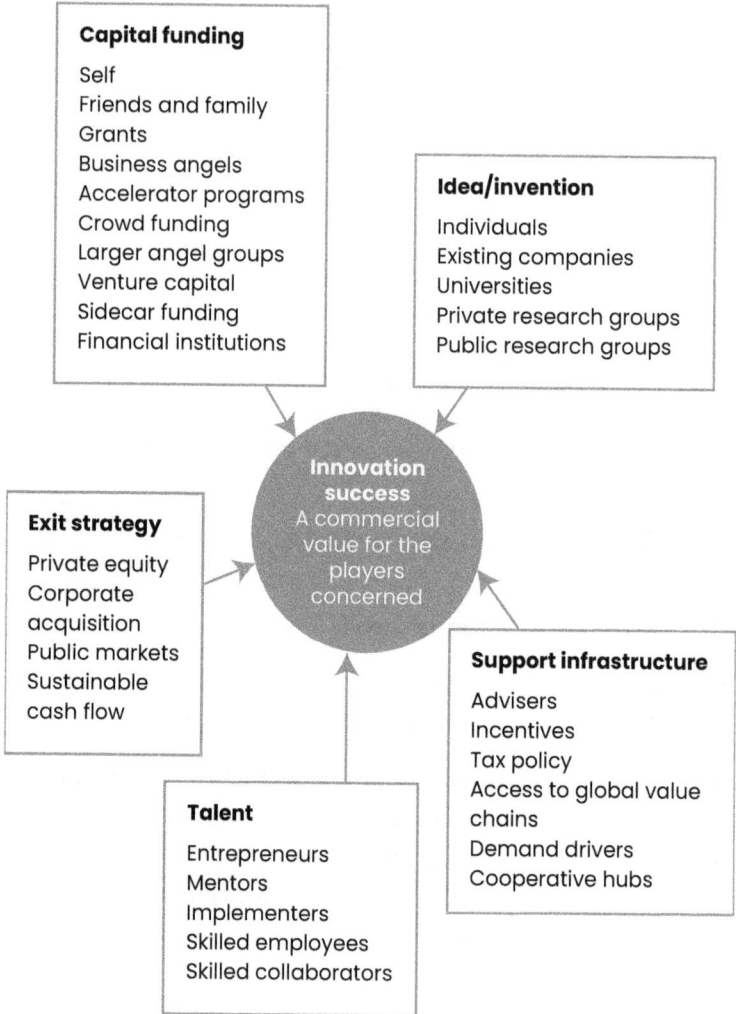

Capital funding

Self
Friends and family
Grants
Business angels
Accelerator programs
Crowd funding
Larger angel groups
Venture capital
Sidecar funding
Financial institutions

Idea/invention

Individuals
Existing companies
Universities
Private research groups
Public research groups

Innovation success
A commercial value for the players concerned

Exit strategy

Private equity
Corporate acquisition
Public markets
Sustainable cash flow

Support infrastructure

Advisers
Incentives
Tax policy
Access to global value chains
Demand drivers
Cooperative hubs

Talent

Entrepreneurs
Mentors
Implementers
Skilled employees
Skilled collaborators

All the groups shown in Figure 1.1 play a vital role in the ecosystem. Their relative importance depends on the nature of the invention and its stage of development.

It is worth expanding on the categories of players to give you an idea of the great value that they add.

Capital funding

Capital is the material wealth used or available for use in the production of more wealth. The examples in Figure 1.1 – self, friends and family, grants, business angels, accelerator programs, crowd funding, larger angel groups, venture capital, sidecar funding and financial institutions – give an idea of where you can access capital funding. At the low end, relying on yourself or friends and family, is a slow and tortured path. The high end of venture capital and financial institutions require you to be at a more mature level and substantially down the innovation path in order to convince them to give you 'other people's money'.

The business angel sits nicely in the middle. Business angels invest their own money and advice and they will help at an earlier stage of commercialising your idea.

Capital, in particular business angel capital, is needed for the following reasons:

► Without capital, most inventions just stay as ideas.
► It provides financial and other resources.
► It shares risk.
► It can lead to you finding mentors and coaches.
► It can be supported by business acumen and governance.
► It can give detailed sector knowledge.

- It can open the doors through networks.

- It will accelerate opportunity if properly used.

Ecosystems that encourage the formation of groups of like capital investors, such as business angel groups and venture capital groups, help add strength and leverage to the capital base.

Sources of ideas and inventions

The starting point of the innovation ecosystem is the invention that might lead to innovation. It can be simply the idea of an individual, it could stem from the operations of an existing business or it could come from the research rigours of a university or research group.

Continual free-flowing ideas feed the system and have the potential to grow innovation. If the other parts of the ecosystem are healthy, then these ideas have a greater chance of commercialisation.

Ecosystems that support and encourage sources of ideas and inventions through a range of activities add great value. Centralisation of grant money, the creation of research hubs, the establishment of forums to bring inventors together and the creation of shared premises are some of the ways that invention can be encouraged.

Support infrastructure

Support infrastructure is a very important enabling factor for invention to turn to innovation. It can come through advisers in areas such as intellectual property (IP), legal, accounting or specialist services. It can come from government incentives, policies or grants, which help reduce risk or increase potential. It can come from a healthy set of demand drivers – economic, social or technical – that propel the customer need for the invention.

Support infrastructure can come through proximity or access to global supply chains or cooperative hubs.

Ecosystems that can leverage national and international infrastructure, as well as build on any unique advantages in the region, can significantly grow the support infrastructure.

Talent

People and their talent play a vitally important role in innovation success. The quality of the entrepreneur means so much, but unless they join forces with quality business implementers, experienced mentors and skilled employees and collaborators, the entrepreneurs' efforts can be wasted.

Ecosystems that build centres of excellence, whether around universities or industry groups, or supply chain hubs or areas of market concentration, can leverage talent considerably.

Exit strategy

An exit strategy in its broadest sense is the only way that an innovation can be monetised. Both the inventor and the investor need to get a clear return for their investment of cash and effort. That is the clear aim of the investors and they require it within a finite timeframe. An angel investor looks for a timeframe of around five years, although that can easily stretch longer and probably move closer to ten years. Monetisation of an innovation can be as simple as a sustainable cash flow so that full or partial funds can be returned to investors. It is more likely to be through a sale to private equity or an acquisition by a larger corporate or by floating on the public markets.

It is important to have a clear idea of your exit strategy well before it is needed to ensure the commercial steps you are taking will directly lead to that exit. The creation of business alliances can also help lead to an effective exit strategy. A healthy ecosystem can usually make those alliances easier to achieve.

Figure 1.2 below takes a simple look at your supply chain and shows some of the potential categories or groups of companies where you might find a partner and finally an exit.

Figure 1.2 – Potential exit partners

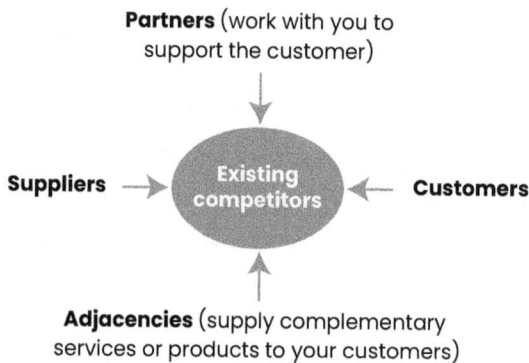

As you move from invention to innovation, your idea matures. The next section gives an overview of that process.

The idea maturity process

Ideas take time to mature and refine so that they genuinely have the potential to become an innovation. Figure 1.3 opposite looks at the stages that are needed from idea generation to established commercialisation. It also indicates the chapters of this book that cover the advice and toolkits that you will find useful at each stage.

Figure 1.3 – Stages for idea generation to commercialisation

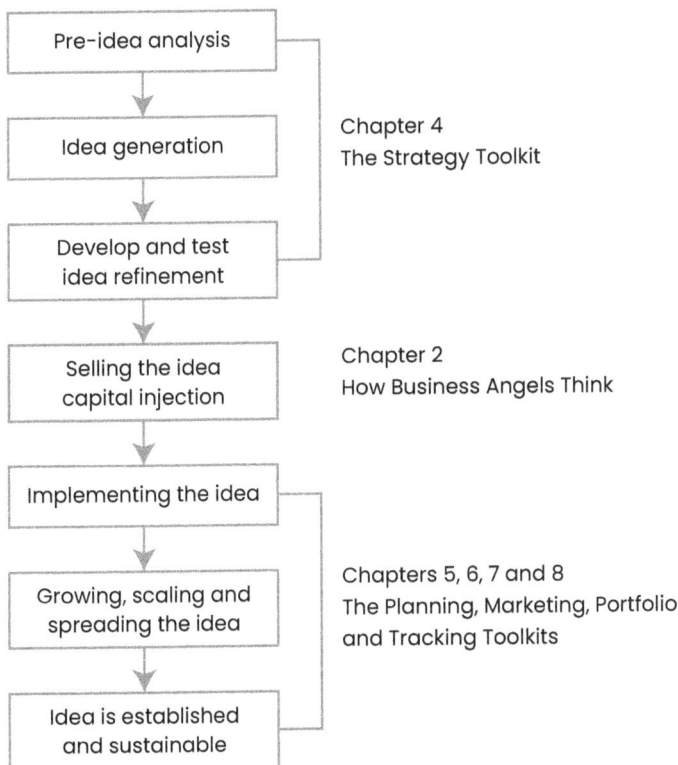

Stages	Chapters
Pre-idea analysis	
Idea generation	Chapter 4 The Strategy Toolkit
Develop and test idea refinement	
Selling the idea capital injection	Chapter 2 How Business Angels Think
Implementing the idea	
Growing, scaling and spreading the idea	Chapters 5, 6, 7 and 8 The Planning, Marketing, Portfolio and Tracking Toolkits
Idea is established and sustainable	

In the next chapter we will take a more detailed look at the business angel. Business angels play such an important role in early-stage capital raising. Understanding their perspective will help you navigate the path to commercialisation.

But before we move to chapter two, let's take a look at the first case study.

Case Study – CSIRO and spin outs

The Commonwealth Scientific and Industrial Research Organisation (CSIRO) is Australia's national science organisation and one of the largest and most diverse scientific research organisations in the world. Its research focuses on the biggest challenges facing the nation and the world. The CSIRO is a source of ideas and invention in Australia's innovation ecosystem.

I had the opportunity to be a CSIRO board member for 10 years and stepped down as the Deputy Chairman in 2016. Their Chief Executive is Dr Larry Marshall, a scientist, technology innovator and business leader. Larry came back to Australia in early 2015 to head up CSIRO after 25 years in the United States.

Over the last century, CSIRO has been the source of so much innovation that it has delivered directly, through technology platforms for industry or through spin out companies.

Laurence Street gives you a glimpse of CSIRO's innovation achievements below.

———————

As Australia's national science agency, CSIRO plays a unique role in the Australian invention-innovation ecosystem as well as the hearts and minds of the Australian people. CSIRO is one of the more recognisable and respected brands in Australia. What CSIRO does is complementary to the work undertaken at universities and other research organisations, but it is differentiated by its purpose and industry focus. CSIRO's mission is two-fold: to carry out scientific research and to encourage or facilitate the application or utilisation of the results of research to benefit Australia.

There are three key pillars to what CSIRO does:

1. It solves the biggest challenges facing our nation and the world.
2. It manages state-of-the-art research facilities on behalf of Australia.
3. It delivers innovation to existing and new business.

Since 1916, CSIRO has advanced Australia with a range of inventions and innovations that has had significant positive impact on the lives of people around the world. During the early years as the Council for Scientific and Industrial Research (CSIR), the organisation was focused on issues concerning our primary industries such as: plant and animal pests and diseases, fuel problems, preservation of foodstuffs and forest products. This focus was later expanded to include: defence radar, building materials, physical metallurgy, wool textiles, coal, climate, environment and land resources.

In 1949, the CSIR was renamed to the modern Commonwealth Scientific and Industrial Research Organisation (CSIRO). Today, over 5,000 talented people work across multiple industry sectors such as ICT, food, agriculture, manufacturing, medical, biotechnology, mining, energy and environment. With our industry and research partners we transform a billion-dollar budget into multi-billion dollar returns for Australia.

Over 100+ years, CSIRO has improved the lives of people everywhere with our inventions. Some of the more well-known are:

- The ubiquitous **WiFi** that we all use today to connect our devices originated from our pioneering work in radioastronomy.

- The **plastic banknotes** that Australia and many other countries use as protection against forgery were developed through research in optically variable devices.

- The **Equivac® HeV vaccine** is used successfully to protect the equine industry against the Hendra virus.

- CSIRO, in collaboration with its partners UNSW and Ciba Vision, developed the **high oxygen permeability polymer materials** that are used in extended wear contact lenses.

- The popular **Aerogard** insect repellent was developed to help protect our troops against mosquitoes in the first and second world wars.

- The CSIRO **Total Wellbeing Diet**, a higher protein, low-fat diet that's nutritious and facilitates sustainable weight loss is a science-based, practical and healthy eating guide that has become a hit amongst the health conscious.

- The Reversible Addition-Fragmentation chain Transfer (**RAFT**) polymerisation technique developed by CSIRO and partners, the global science company DuPont, has revolutionised the way industry can control the production of high quality, new and unique plastics.

- Boasting four times the resistant starch and twice the dietary fibre of regular grains, the low GI supergrain, **BARLEYmax™** developed by CSIRO using GM free processes is now used in a range of commercially available food products, as well as being recognised by international health bodies.

- In the 1960s, CSIRO developed a **self-twisting yarn process** and a new generation of spinning machines with Repco Ltd to speed up the rate wool can be spun into yarn, without breaking the wool or reducing the strength of the yarn.

- On a similar theme, partnering with the Royal Melbourne Hospital's Central Linen Service, CSIRO developed **Softly®** detergent, the first formula to successfully wash wool at high temperatures, killing bacteria while not shrinking the wool. This innovation has been successfully commercialised by global personal care company Unilever with the Softy® brand still available in supermarkets today.

Each year, six of CSIRO's technologies alone contribute over $5 billion to the economy in areas as diverse as biosecurity, water management, building energy, automated mining, advanced materials and aquaculture.

Our more recent commercialisation successes include:

- The **ColoSTAT™**, a simple blood test for screening technology for the detection of colorectal cancer that is being commercialised by Rhythm BioSciences Ltd.

- The **WindScape** software used by Windlab Systems Pty Ltd for broad area, high resolution wind mapping and capable of mapping vast areas at a resolution of 100m or better was originally developed by CSIRO.

- Amfora, Inc. has partnered with CSIRO to commercialise a technology that significantly increases oil production in plants, including vegetative tissues, such as stems and leaves. This technology, initially directed toward improving the efficiency of producing biofuel feedstocks in plants, will be applied to increasing the energy density in forage crops by Amfora.

- Chrysos Corporation was established by CSIRO and a group of investors to commercialise **PhotonAssay**, a high energy minerals characterisation technique that provides a rapid, chemistry-free approach to material analysis in the mining industry, which significantly improves both absolute accuracy and sensitivity of minerals such as gold and silver to very low concentrations.

- Titomic Ltd was established to commercialise CSIRO's process for the application of **cold-gas dynamic spraying of titanium** or titanium alloy particles onto a scaffold to produce load-bearing structures with improved properties.

Laurence Street, 2018, CSIRO Board Secretary and GM, Commercial and Governance

CHAPTER TWO
HOW BUSINESS ANGELS THINK

Each year, billions of dollars of investment around the world supports fledgling companies introducing their inventions to the market. Angel investment as a category exceeds the seed and early-stage venture capital contribution. It is the primary source of external seed and early-stage equity financing in many countries. There are angel groups and associations in most countries.

What do angel investors do?

Business angel investors invest their own money, strategic and operational expertise and personal networks into new ventures. They are not investing 'other people's money'. The notion of angel investment has been around for centuries, but the sector is becoming far more sophisticated with the growing number of angel groups and angel networks that exist in many regions and many industries.

Business angels are high net worth individuals, usually with business experience, who are classified as sophisticated investors. Each country has its own way of enabling sophisticated investors to register themselves. Angels tend to invest in a portfolio of companies to spread the risk. For each investment they usually provide somewhere between $25,000 to $500,000 depending on the capital intensity of the industry, the size of their group and the nature of the idea. They either invest as individuals or as an angel group depending on their wealth and the size of the investment required.

Angel investors play an important role in economic growth, technology leaps and the success of what otherwise is just an invention. The substantial reduction in technology costs, particularly over the last decade, has allowed lower cost capital start-up requirements which, in turn, has allowed the business angel sector to grow.

The business angel perspective

Any investment in early-stage inventions is a risky business and business angels realise that. They therefore try to find ways to minimise their risk. They recognise that the risk is high but that a great innovation might be created for both themselves and society. Angel investors, particularly angel groups, try to optimise their chance of success in the following ways by:

► ensuring there is a good mix of expertise in their investment group;

► investing in areas of technology or industry where there is reasonable experience;

► setting clear pitch criteria for inventors;

► undertaking significant due diligence;

► investing in a portfolio of businesses to minimise risk; and

► joining and contributing to a well-functioning innovation ecosystem.

Building these optimising techniques around the investments doesn't assure angel investors of success but it at least increases their chances. As the inventor, if you are to get capital support from angel investors, you will need to understand their perspective and be sure you give them the confidence and information they require.

Aligning yourself with the right business angels

You are more likely to gain capital investment from an angel group if your invention lines up with the expertise and criteria that this group has set themselves. So you need to do some homework before you approach an angel group. You should try to understand the following:

► What investments do they already have and does your invention somehow complement these?

► Do they only invest in a particular technology area or a particular industry?

► Are they strong participators in their innovation ecosystem?

► Do they align themselves with specific idea generators (such as universities) or investor groups?

► Do they prefer investing in a particular region?

► Do they prefer smaller or larger capital investment ideas?

► Do they have clear pitch criteria and guidelines?

► Do they have a demonstrated success rate?

► Do they already know any of your key collaborator team?

Once you have considered the above you will have some idea of whether their areas of interest fit with the nature of your business idea. If you can pick a well aligned angel group, then your chance of capital investment success has already been increased.

Don't underestimate the value of aligning yourself with the right partner.

Getting to the pitch

You have now found some target angel groups that you would like to engage with. Usually they will ask you to supply some preliminary information before they invite you to pitch your idea to them. Most angel groups have a website or a contact person and they will give you a set of questions to answer or a list of information to supply. If you don't have the answers to these questions or have not thought about this information, then it means you have a lot more analysis to undertake about your business idea before you formally ask for investment.

What these groups usually need to learn from their preliminary questions are:

- a clear and simple explanation of your product, service or idea;
- any IP or know-how protection that you have;
- an indication that your idea is scalable either nationally or internationally;
- an assurance that you at least have a basic business and financial plan in place; and
- an indication of how much money you need.

The pitch

The opportunity to put your business idea to a single investor or group of angel investors is a clear milestone in the commercialisation of your invention. You will usually only have up to five minutes to make this pitch and get the interest that leads to good questions and follow up.

This opportunity should not be wasted. Do not do it too early. Make sure you really have thought through your business idea and its appeal to the market. Make sure you have gathered clear and unambiguous facts and data. Make sure you have enough experience in your team to convince angel investors that you can implement this great idea.

In my experience, there are many approaches you can use to convince investors, but a clear, logical, defensible approach is the best. Here are what I think are the essential elements of your pitch, which I will describe in more detail below:

► Your team and idea
► The target market
► The market gap
► Your solution
► Your value proposition
► Your business model
► Your business plan and timeframe
► The pre-value and investment needed
► The capital plan
► The exit strategy.

Your team and idea

In my experience, a good idea with an energetic, competent team to implement it is a far better proposition than a great idea with a less competent team. It is important that in your pitch you:

► describe your idea simply and briefly;

- present a team with a track record of implementation and with a set of skills that are relevant to the idea that you are trying to commercialise; and

- present the direct associates in your venture and any strategic partners that you intend to use.

These components can add great credibility to your idea and increase the probability of investors having confidence in you.

It is essential you choose and present your team well.

Target market

Knowing your target market is crucial to the commercial success of your invention or idea. You need to be able to address the following questions as this gives an indication of the commercial attractiveness of the market for your idea:

- What is the size and scale of the market you are interested in?

- Is it growing at an attractive rate?

- Does it have room for new competitors?

- Does it have accessible paths to market?

Market gap

Another consideration is whether there is a clear market gap? You need to show that there is an area of demand in the market that is not being met. Any research that can support this market gap is very valuable and adds weight to your pitch. You need to be able to estimate the size of the gap and scale and link this to your invention. A simple graphical presentation to illustrate this is best.

Your solution

You must be able to describe your solution to the market gap in a clear and logical way. In supporting your solution wherever possible, you need to call on appropriate facts and data or market research. Results of a pilot project with your solution can be very helpful at this point in your pitch.

Value proposition

You must be able to describe the value that your idea or invention gives to the market. What would customers see as a feature that they would pay for? Is there a pain or pleasure point?

Business model

This is where you describe how your idea can be commercialised. You need to explain your path to market and if it is a proven path. You need to be able to explain the value to the customer and how they see and pay for that value. Your investors need to understand the points where customers will pay and the timeframe in which your idea makes revenue and then profit. This is a real point of credibility testing for angel investors. If there is no clear path to market, there is little hope for your business idea.

Business plan

Your business plan should have the detail of your assumptions about the implementation of your idea. It should have a projection of your profit and loss and cash flow over the next few years, with any milestones highlighted. Your business plan should show your present position and how you will proceed both without and with the invested funds.

You should be able to discuss and defend the underlying assumptions in your business plan.

Pre-value and investment needed

Your pre-value is the underlying value of your business idea if you continue with the funds you already have. It is what you believe your business idea would be valued at before the investment dollars you are now asking for. You can then introduce the new investment required and how that would grow the value of your business idea. Your pre-value and the value of the investment you require determines the percentage ownership that your investor group would have.

Your pre-value should be derived from your business plan assumptions. If you have a clear view of, or can make defensible assumptions about your future cash flows, then you can determine your net present value (NPV). This is described in detail in chapter four. Many a time in early stage investment the pre-value is very subjective. If you do not have positive cash flow, then your revenue is an indicator of your value. Your rule of thumb valuation can be between five to ten times your revenue depending on your annual growth rate and your revenue timeframe. Your pre-valuation needs to have some stretch but still be realistic or you will lose investors at this point.

Capital plan

Your capital plan describes how you will spend the investment given to you. You might need to spend it on marketing and sales, production enhancement, further research and development (R&D), partner engagement or any combination of the above.

You need to be specific and show how this investment is what is really needed at your stage of commercialisation. Your capital plan should be specific and prioritised. It should also have a time-frame for drawdowns if you require the funding in a few stages.

Exit strategy

Your exit strategy is another critical point for the investor to consider. It allows them to understand when and how they will get a return on their investment. It could be through acquisition, merger with a key partner, a public float or a management buyout. Your exit strategy needs to be credible and you should give an early identification of some of the players involved and the time-frame. This information does not need to be comprehensive, but you do need to show that you have thought about it.

Pitch preparation

Giving a pitch to investors is a highly stressful experience so do not underestimate the stress you will feel. In order to reduce at least some of that stress and ensure a professional touch to your presentation you need to:

- ► have a few practice runs to be happy with the content and time it takes to make the pitch;
- ► get to the location where you are making your pitch early so you are not rushing;
- ► make sure you have had enough food and hydration before the meeting;
- ► wear appropriate business clothing;
- ► test any technology that you will use in your pitch;
- ► have enough hard copy handouts;
- ► ask for questions to be at the end of your pitch and decide who on your team will answer what type of questions.

Pitch example

Using the ten areas above I have sketched out a notional, high-level pitch example. It consists of 10 pages. This is about the amount of information you need to get your story across in an efficient and enticing manner. Your pitch needs to sell the clear business opportunity without being too detailed and boring.

You obviously need to have done your homework and have back-up information. You also need to be able to defend your position with facts and data.

Be prepared for questions but if you don't know the answer, say so. You can always follow up after the meeting and give your investors a more considered answer – this will give you a second bite of the cherry.

This pitch example below will at least start you off on the road to investor presentations. You may want to use it as a checklist to see that you have covered the essential points, when you are preparing for your own pitch. The unique nature of your idea or invention might require some other complementary slides.

Angel investors use their head and their heart. They expect a well thought out business strategy and approach. They do also get personally involved so if your idea has some flare and happens to pull their heartstrings, you might get an emotional response as well. I hope this provides some help to you as a basic framework and good luck in preparing your own pitch.

Example pitch – SLIDE 1

Our great idea – investor pitch

Our company

Our company has been operating successfully on a small scale but we now have a product that has the potential to grow the company and transform the market.

Our team

We have an experienced management team and some trusted advisers and investors.

Management team:

- person #1
- person #2
- person #3
- person #4

Key advisers and investors:

- #1
- #2

Example pitch –SLIDE 2

Our market is both large and attractive ...

Target market $80 billion by 2023

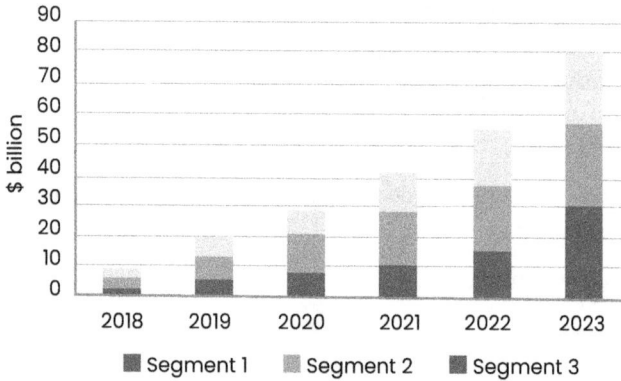

Key market attractiveness

- High growth
- Room for new competitors
- Attractive margins
- Diversity of segments

Example pitch – SLIDE 3

There is a clear market gap in ...

Research comments and statistics

- Market needs
- Points to the top right quadrant

Competitive landscape

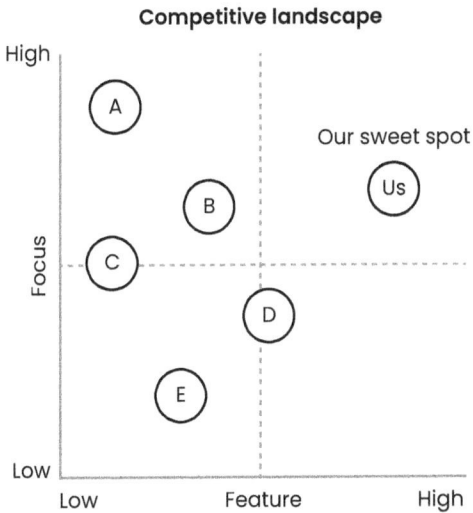

We are well positioned to differentiate ourselves.

Example pitch – SLIDE 4

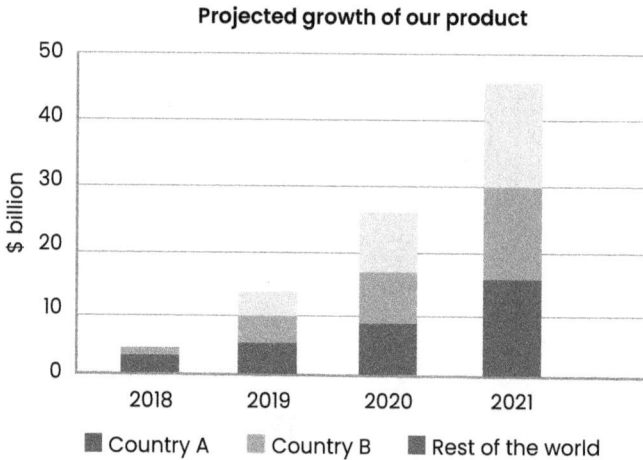

Our solution fills that market gap ...

Key features

- Simple description
- Potential global reach
- Intellectual property strength
- Why now?

Potential demand

Example pitch – SLIDE 5

Our value proposition is strong ...

Pain removed and pleasure provided

- Pain points
- Simple solution
- Customer value analysis

Pilot introduction feedback

- Description
- Customer statistics
- Customer comments

Example pitch – SLIDE 6

Our business model is proven ...

Supply chain map

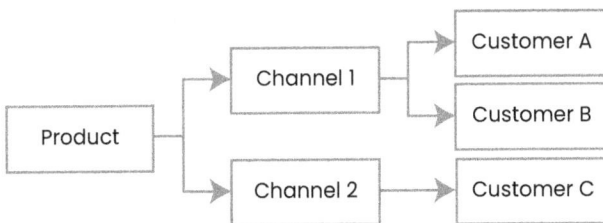

Payment points

- Initial purchase
- Advice
- Maintenance and support

Example pitch – SLIDE 7

Our business plan is achievable ...

Key business plan components

- Revenue targets
- Cost assumptions
- P&L and cash flow projections
- Capital injections
- Employee recruitment
- Other key milestones
- Show potential before and after angel investment

Example pitch – SLIDE 8

We have strong pre-value, but your investment will give you a share in further upside ...

Our present NPV (pre-value)

- Relate back to business plan assumptions
- Assume only capital injection that you can do without further investors

Capital investment required

- Detail of the capital investment required
- Indication of any staging of capital
- Indication of what might come from other investor groups

Share of business

- Indication of % share offered for the capital investment (this should be a ratio of the capital invested and the pre-value)

Example pitch – SLIDE 9

Our capital investment plan is sound and prioritised ...

Details of area of spend

- Marketing and sales
- Intellectual property protection
- Product enhancement
- Production facilities

Details of timing of spend

- Spend details over the next few years
- Potential staging of investment

Example pitch – SLIDE 10

We have a viable exit strategy for investors ...

Key messages

- Potential options investigated
- Fit with business plan
- Key partners for the future
- Timeframe to exit

Thank you for your attention

- We have much detail behind this presentation
- Happy to follow up now or later with any questions

Questions?

After the pitch

You are at the stage where you have given your five-minute pitch and answered all the potential investors' questions. You now leave the room and await some feedback. There are two possibilities: the angel investors will either have no interest or they will want to follow up some more.

If they have no interest, ask what the key reasons were. If you can correct any issues, do so and try again with this group. If it is clear you are not aligned with this group, then take any lessons from the experience and pitch to another group that might be more aligned to your idea. Not many pitch participants get it right first time. It can be an iterative process. As with most life-changing moments, you need to be persistent.

If you have an angel group that is interested and wants to follow up in more detail, then this is where the hard part really starts. Here are some of the follow-ups that could occur:

► There is an interest in your idea but a tough negotiation around the pre-value. You need to listen to the comments, defend your position with facts and data, and look at it from their perspective to come to an agreed pre-value. If you think this group's view is really wrong, then you should try other investors, but you need to make an honest assessment of your own valuation.

► Once you come to an agreement on the pre-value, then the percentage ownership of the investors will fall out depending on the capital they are prepared to invest.

► There could be significant negotiation around the capital required and the timing of capital injections. You need to be able to show that you are spending capital wisely and efficiently.

► There could be negotiation about the level of angel support and advice. Angels typically have great commercial experience and strong networks. You should look at how you can best utilise them. It could be worthwhile having the relevant angel investor on your advisory board or even your company board. This personal involvement in the business idea is the key advantage of using angel investors.

► There could be discussion around refining and finalising your business plan and the key milestones that you are prepared to set. These milestones can sometimes be used as a gate if the capital injection is staged. They assume a reasonable achievement of goals before more capital is invested.

► There is likely to be discussion about the method and timing of reporting back to investors. This is a reasonable request. It is customary for investors to receive a quarterly report on the progress of the venture and how their capital has been used.

► There is also likely to be some serious discussion around the appropriate exit strategy and its timing. Angel investors are usually very patient. They quite rightly want a return on their investment, but they like to see a business grow to considerable potential before that happens. They are, however, an early stage investor, so this typically puts them in the 5 to 10-year range.

All of the discussion points above lead to the development of a term sheet. This is a legal document between the investors and the company. In the next section I will discuss the term sheet and give you an idea of the typical format in which the term sheet might be presented to you. Obviously when entering into a term sheet with investors, you should get the appropriate legal advice.

Term sheets

Term sheets can take many forms and can be specific to the nature of the investment and the venture. The document will typically have component sections and refer to detailed schedules in the back of the document. In trying to give an overview of term sheets, I've tried to cover the typical components you are likely to see in one. This will give you some idea of what to think about and prepare for.

Some of the typical sections of a term sheet are as follows:

- Conditions precedent
- The offering or investment overview
- The share or investor rights
- Governance structures
- Milestones and staging of investment
- Shareholder participation and reporting requirements
- Exit preparation.

I will now take you through an explanation of each one of these sections of the term sheet.

Conditions precedent

Sometimes there might be some due diligence investigations required by investors before the term sheet finally takes effect and these will be included in the conditions precedent section. It could be that some structural changes need to be made before the term sheet is accepted. These changes could be intellectual property being transferred into the company, founders and key employees entering into employment contracts with the company, a new constitution being enacted that sets out certain shareholder rights or simply that investors are satisfied with their detailed due diligence.

The offering or investment overview

This section specifically describes the essence of the agreement. It typically covers the parties involved, the investment amount, the share price, the general use of funds, the pre and post money valuation and the share capital structure. It will probably have some schedules associated with it to give more detail and specific shareholder information.

The share or investor rights

This section gives detail around the rights of an investor. It follows the principles of fairness for initial and minority shareholders to not be disadvantaged by any future arrangements of the company. It typically covers subscription share rights, pre-emptive rights, drag along rights, tag along rights and investor control rights. It tries to cover the range of events that can occur and how shareholders will be treated.

Governance structures

This section defines some clear governance principles around how the company will operate in the interests of shareholders. It covers board structure, board meetings, observer status of investors, executive and non-executive director fees, primary board responsibilities and the review of business plans and budgets.

Milestones and staging of investment

Some agreements have staged investments. The initial shareholding will relate to stage one of the investment at a particular share price. There could be an arrangement with investors to contribute at further stages of investment when specific milestones are reached. These milestones could be the development of a production line or the establishment of a market in a new country or acceptance by a regulating authority. If the achievement of these milestones grows the value of the company then the next stage investment might be agreed to be at a higher share price. There would normally be a schedule attached to the term sheet that describes the milestones in detail, the next stage investment and at what share price this would be.

Investor participation and reporting requirements

If this is not covered in enough detail in the governance section, there could be a specific section on investor participation and reporting requirements. This would cover investor participation in an advisory board or on the company board and the details of reporting requirements to investors.

Exit preparation

This section would not necessarily be too specific, but it would recognise the facts that investors are there to get a return and need to have a path to exit to realise that return. It would create an obligation on the board of the company to investigate viable exit options for investors in a reasonable timeframe.

* * * * *

Once you and your investors have finally agreed on the term sheet, then you have moved from creating and selling an invention or business idea to running a business to commercialise your idea. If the market accepts it in a material way then, congratulations, you have created an innovation.

The next chapter moves on to the next part of your journey. It covers the essential tools you need to manage a business from strategic review to day-to-day management.

Case Study – SWOOP Analytics

SWOOP Analytics was formed in 2014 by Laurence Lock Lee and Cai and Marianne Kjaer. It is an Australian company based in Sydney with people on the ground in the UK and US. By analysing data from a variety of sources they provide employees and management with unique insights to make informed and evidence-based decisions about collaboration and the health of their social networks.

SWOOP is the result of more than 10 years of consulting experience in mapping organisational networks. Based on more than 100 projects they have identified the most compelling and valuable metrics that help organisations drive collaborative business performance.

Below is the SWOOP story in Laurence Lock Lee's own words

———————

Unlike the archetype 'light bulb' idea moment, our SWOOP Analytics story is more of a slow burn one, going back over nearly two decades. I met Cai Kjaer in 2000, just post the dotcom bust. I was leading a knowledge management consulting practice for global IT company CSC (Computer Sciences Corporation). I was joined by a young and energetic Cai, from Denmark, looking for a slightly larger and definitely warmer pool to play in. At that time, knowledge management was being described as a combination of 'connections' and 'collections', with 90% of the interest in it focused on electronic artefacts, document management systems and the like.

I had now discovered the largely academic discipline of social network analysis (SNA) that focused precisely on my interests in the 'connections' part of knowledge management. Running a few projects at BHP Ltd before introducing SNA to other clients, I found a more than willing apprentice in Cai, who quickly caught the SNA bug.

SNA projects typically collect their data via surveys, but we always had an interest in deriving relationship insights indirectly through digital activity tracking. Some early projects tracking connections via email discussions and knowledge sharing systems exposed the promise of developing relationship-centred insights from how people actually worked and connected, more so than how they thought they worked and connected.

I took a deep dive into the academic sources by undertaking a part-time PhD, researching how a firm's social capital could contribute to their share market performance. Cai mined third party market data to feed his SNA of a market place. For his part, Cai became excited about how companies were connected via shared board membership and the insights that could be derived from this interconnected network of board members. He devoted a whole Easter holiday period holed up in the NSW State Library, manually mining board data from published annual reports.

In 2006, Cai and I took the big step of creating our first start-up, Optimice, to focus on bringing SNA consulting to the commercial world. We took advantage of meeting up with an experienced government sponsored start-up adviser, who promptly advised us that our start-up idea, as a niche consultancy, would never scale; this was a big dose of cold water! Undeterred though we pushed on and even built our own SNA survey tool product, in partnership with a fellow CSC refugee and tech head Paul Williamson. Regrettably, our initial start-up adviser proved right. Optimice couldn't scale. Despite having a continuous number of blue chip clients around the world, as a strategic niche consultancy, Optimice became a start-up investors call the living dead.

In 2014, a pivot from a consulting firm to product firm saw a new start-up, SWOOP Analytics. By this time Facebook, Twitter and LinkedIn had brought social networking to the consumer world. Another start-up, Yammer, was targeting social networking inside the enterprise and was being acquired by Microsoft.

Having conducted a number of experiments mining Yammer for relationships, we felt the market timing was right to bring real time SNA to the enterprise market with early analytics sourced directly from our Optimice work.

A former knowledge management contact, now at Microsoft, introduced us to Macquarie Bank who were disappointed in the analytics provided by Yammer. We pitched our relationship-centred analytics and they were sold. We now had the impetus (and further funds) to build out the SWOOP product, which was ready in 2015.

With the help of Microsoft things moved quickly with both Westpac and Telstra (both ASX top five companies) committing to SWOOP. At Westpac, the CEO was particularly impressed by SWOOP's ability to model online behaviours, presenting them as 'personas' on a personal dashboard. All procurement records were broken and we even developed a custom dashboard for the CEO to monitor the collaborative behaviours of his senior executive leaders. Importantly, we also now had a story to pitch to potential investors.

Having already experienced one start-up, we were acutely aware of how crowded the start-up advice market was, with the majority of players looking to help spend other people's money. We made an early decision to look for angel investors who invested their own money but at the same time could provide us with wise counsel based on their real-world experience either as leaders of major corporations or entrepreneurs in their own right. What's more, we chose to live by our own principles and network our way into the angel investor groups. We connected with two angel investors.

Eileen Doyle was a Director of Hunter Angels and a former BHP colleague of mine. The Hunter Angels have 'industrial' roots', with experience from the types of customers SWOOP would be selling into.

Marcus Dawe is a member of Canberra Capital Angels. Marcus was a colleague from CSC after his start-up was acquired by them.

The Capital Angels and Marcus brought tech start-up experience. We were successful in our first round capital raising with both.

Interestingly, our fill-in-the-form pitch to Sydney Angels didn't even pass the first filter. There is something to be said about working your relationships!

In 2017, we added a Workplace by Facebook as an additional revenue line to our Yammer business, which is now growing nicely. What's more, both Microsoft and Facebook can see the value of SWOOP inside their own respective organisations and are now actively promoting SWOOP to their internal stakeholders.

SWOOP in 2018 is quickly approaching $1 million in revenue from close to 50 customers, from an increasingly global market, and we are cash flow positive to boot! Selling to the enterprise, however, can be hard work. Procurement cycles are long and going global from a welcoming local market is challenging for a small start-up. But we are growing! Our technical team has grown from one (Paul Williamson, our Optimice partner) to three and we now have partnering and customer service staff covering North America and Europe.

On the research front we have worked with the University of Sydney and the University of Griffith to add scientific rigour to elements of our work. We have just jointly published our first journal article with Stanford University, who have used SWOOP data and insights to illustrate how gender diversity and inclusion can be monitored in real time.

While we have, at times, allowed ourselves to entertain the thought of a dream exit, Eileen is nailing our feet to the ground. 'That is a good start. But to get any serious attention you need to be at least $10 million revenue!' she told us. 'Have you updated your business plan? Have you articulated your ecosystem and identified all potential acquirers? What about your future lines of revenue? Will they get you to $10 million?'

It's one thing to think big and reach for the stars. It's another thing to make sure you are on the stairway to get there. Isn't that what Angels are for?

Dr Laurence Lock Lee, 2018, SWOOP Founder and Chief Scientist

CHAPTER THREE
BASIC BUSINESS MANAGEMENT

The last 20 years have seen significant changes in factors that have made the external environment for businesses far less stable. Among other factors there has been globalisation of markets, a significant increase in worldwide competition, a greater propensity for substitute materials, reduced barriers to entry and increased access to markets through lower cost technologies and far less stability in financial markets.

In these fast-changing times, business leaders and managers are driven to find quick fixes and superficial solutions. Many don't take or have the time to understand their business drivers. This makes the continued performance of their business even worse and they become less competitive. A focus on the short term means all the energy of the organisation is devoted to crisis management. This, in turn, means many may fall behind or are simply not interested in the basic understanding and management of their business in times of rapid, technology-driven change. This is a major trap and business leaders must avoid it at all costs. They must use appropriate tools wisely at the right stage in their business. They must have a full understanding of their business environment, strategic direction and day-to-day management.

These comments apply just as much to those in a start-up company or those in a company launching a major new invention.

There is no quick solution for a business. And once this principle is accepted, business leaders can get back to the basics of understanding and then running their organisations for the longer term, building value and a sustainable business.

Get back to basics

As your business idea matures and you are in the process of implementing it, you are back to the basic principles of running a business. This is not as glamorous as idea creation, but it is where commercialisation happens. Getting back to basics means doing all the necessary things to ensure both short-term and long-term performance. It means putting disciplines in place that ensure all areas of the business are considering both strategic and day-to-day issues. It means ensuring all areas of the business are heading towards a common, constant purpose.

A good understanding of your business environment and constancy of purpose are key factors for a successful business.

Five toolkits of business performance management

Figure 3.1 highlights five toolkits of business performance management. A chapter of this book will be devoted to each toolkit.

Figure 3.1 – Five toolkits of business performance management

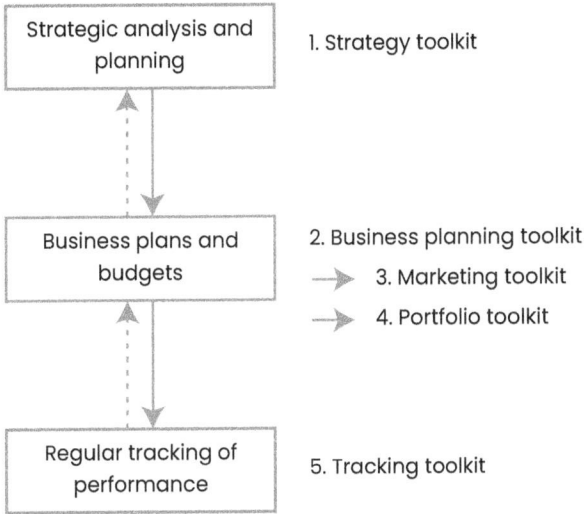

Strategic analysis and planning	1. Strategy toolkit
Business plans and budgets	2. Business planning toolkit 3. Marketing toolkit 4. Portfolio toolkit
Regular tracking of performance	5. Tracking toolkit

1. **The strategy toolkit** is essential to ensure the development and maintenance of a sustainable competitive advantage. Strategic analysis and planning has a long-term focus. You need to undertake these activities in detail every couple of years or when there are major changes to industry and economic factors that might affect your business. You also need to check any major decisions your business is taking against the logic of your strategic analysis and strategic direction.

2. **The business planning toolkit** is vital for setting short-term and measurable targets. These targets are usually prepared every year with clear action plans to ensure things happen. Annual results provide feedback on your strategic analysis and planning.

Depending on the nature and complexity of your business, the next three toolkits will be needed in whole or in part.

3. **The marketing toolkit** describes your potential, positions your products and provides direction to sales staff.

4. **The portfolio toolkit** helps manage a range of development activities in the interests of the total business.

5. **The tracking toolkit** helps provide you with the few key performance measures that tell you if you are on track with your plan.

It sounds simple and as we get into each toolkit you will see a lot of common sense.

What it takes to run a business well is the discipline to undertake these steps with rigour and honesty.

CHAPTER FOUR
THE STRATEGY TOOLKIT

Before I introduce you to the strategy toolkit, let me remind you of my definitions of strategic analysis and strategic planning.

Strategic analysis is a high-level analysis of the factors that influence your areas of business. It also includes an analysis of your company's position with respect to competitors. That is, what is the industry's position and where does your company fit?

Strategic planning is the development of the long-term direction of your company and key strategies that deliver long-term success.

Competent strategic analysis and planning are essential to ensure the development and maintenance of a sustainable competitive advantage.

Strategic analysis tools

When conducting a strategic analysis of your business environment, there are many methodologies you can use. I have found the following five tools the most useful in assisting me to form a strategic direction:

1. Environmental analysis tool
2. Industry attractiveness tool
3. SWOT analysis tool
4. Competitor analysis tool
5. Customer analysis tool.

In describing these strategy tools, I will give an overview and a suggested layout to summarise the analysis in your reporting.

Environmental analysis

In a nutshell, environmental analysis is the identification of the specific external factors that most heavily impact on your company's costs, sales, operations and/or profitability.

These specific external factors could be, for example, economic conditions, technology developments, government policies or customer preferences. These factors by definition cannot be controlled, but you can prepare for them and counter their impact. A proactive approach, where possible, should be taken to influence them and to prepare your business to optimise performance in the face of them.

As well as identifying external factors, it is also worth quantifying them. A clear identification of factors can help you determine the most likely scenario for your business and a range of possible scenarios. Acknowledging this range of possible scenarios allows you to develop alternative strategies as a backup and to fully develop your strategy for the most likely scenario.

Table 4.1 is a notional environmental analysis for a business. It places high, medium or low ratings on the probability of that factor occurring. It also attempts to quantify the impact the factor may have on the business.

Obviously, your own analysis can be far more detailed. You can also decide which external factor assumptions will form part of your base case for your strategic plan.

It is helpful as well to consider the mix of external factors and debate them with your team to come up with a key conclusion for your business.

Table 4.1 – Environmental analysis example

External factor	Probability	Impact on business
New government tax policy	High	10% revenue reduction 20% reduction in profit
New government environmental policy	Medium	10% increase in costs
New competitor technology	Low	40% revenue reduction
10% increase in US exchange rate	Medium	10% net profit reduction
Customers require delivery in half the time	High	20% increase in short-term costs Major operational changes
Customer A and Customer B merge	Medium	10% revenue reduction Closure of region C

Key conclusions: Our external threats at present outweigh our external opportunities.

Industry attractiveness

It is vital to understand the underlying competitive factors in the industry sector in which your company operates. You need a clear understanding of the attractiveness of your industry and your company's position within this industry. To arrive at this understanding you can follow the basic line of questioning shown in Figure 4.1.

Figure 4.1 – Industry attractive analysis

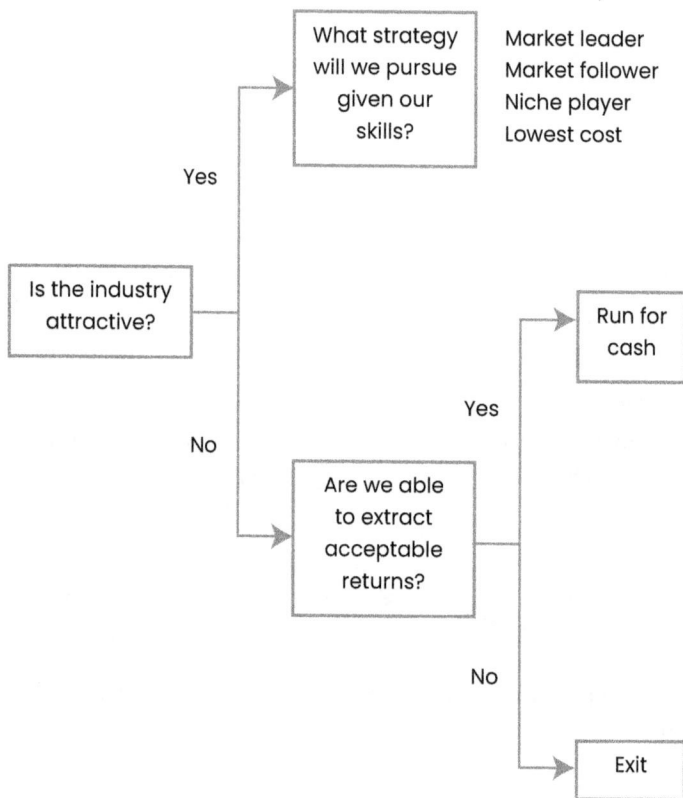

A detailed industry analysis is a massive task that takes many months to complete. Depending on the detail you feel you need, you might pull this together yourself or pay for some of it to be done. It will be money or effort well spent as it is the basis of understanding the industry your business is part of. For your industry, you need to judge the level of detail required. There is a wide range of groups that provide an information source:

► Industry observers
► Your employees
► Service providers
► Customers
► Suppliers.

From this information gleaned from these sources, you can begin to look at industry attractiveness.

A number of standard attractiveness criteria can be used to determine general industry attractiveness. The criteria that I use are:

► Growth
► Size
► Profitability
► Competitive structure
► Market diversity
► Cyclicability
► Community risk.

It is almost impossible to find an industry that has high positive attractiveness in every one of these areas, but an analysis of each area will give you a balanced view of the attractiveness of your industry. The analysis will also help you in defining strategies to manage any less attractive components of your industry.

I will now take you through the thought processes to assess your industry with respect to these criteria.

Growth

Growth potential is not just about increasing sales of individual products or services. It is about understanding the factors that drive demand for your range of products or services, i.e. your product sector or service sector. Understanding these factors will allow you to determine the growth potential of your business.

You will need to understand the typical consumers of your products or services and any factors that influence growth or a reduction in the number of consumers. Some typical factors to consider could be:

- Demographic trends
- Social trends
- Technology trends.

Demographic trends refer to changes in age profiles, sex, geographic movements, etc. For example, if people over 55 mainly use your services, then your growth potential is probably high, given that the percentage of over 55s continues to increase every year. You are part of a growing industry.

Social trends refer to changes in the mix of work and leisure, or changes in the typical activities people perform in their lives. For example, if your business is primarily concerned with selling prepared meals, then your growth potential is probably high, given the increasing trend towards buying these products. You again are part of a growing industry.

Technology trends in this context refer to the introduction of new mass technology that allows people to conduct activities that were otherwise technically impossible or too expensive. For example, if your business is directly related to the number of personal devices, or the number of internet connections, then your growth potential is probably high given the increasing mass availability of this technology. You again are part of a growing industry.

From an attractiveness point of view, industries whose future growth predictions exceed average gross domestic product (GDP) growth are obviously the winners. A simple categorisation of growth can just be:

- ► Low (below GDP)
- ► Medium (at or slightly above GDP)
- ► High (obviously above GDP).

Size

Industry size is an important criterion. Once an industry reaches substantial size it allows a diversity of competition. It encourages technical innovators, supermarket style, base product, geographically-based and single-product companies all to participate in the market. This provides wider choice for customers and different strategy options for companies.

The actual size in revenue an industry needs to reach to have the right critical mass to promote diversity of competition will depend on the capital intensity of the industry. The lower the capital required to enter an industry, the lower the revenue base required for an individual company will be.

A good example of appropriate industry size is a comparison of the fast food industry to a capital-intensive manufacturing industry. A prospective owner looking at a fast food business, with a relatively low capital input, would only need to consider the demand and revenue base from their local suburb. A prospective owner of a capital-intensive manufacturing business would need to consider national and perhaps international demand for their products to ensure they can develop a high enough revenue base.

A simple categorisation of size can just be:

- ► Below target
- ► Above target (the size at a critical level for a competitor to enter).

Profitability/returns

Fundamentally attractive industries are those where the average return on funds employed is greater than the average cost of funds.

The bigger the difference, the more attractive an industry is. In these industries wealth is being created. Of course, risk and return are related and the higher the return, the greater the risk.

To calculate return on funds employed (ROFE), simply divide earnings before interest and tax (EBIT) by total funds employed and multiply by 100 to make a percentage. Figure 4.2 below gives some very simple assumptions and calculates the minimum ROFE for wealth creation.

Unfortunately, an analysis of the last few decades for a number of mature manufacturing industries would show the average return on funds employed at less than the average cost of funds. These industries have not been attractive. It does not mean the particular companies at the top of the industry cannot earn acceptable returns, but it does mean that a lot of companies are not earning acceptable returns.

Figure 4.2 – Calculating minimum ROFE for wealth creation

Minimum ROFE = WACC/(1 – Tax Rate)

e.g. 16.7% = 10.7%/(1 – 36%)

*WACC is the weighted average cost of capital (after tax).
It is calculated as follows:

After-tax cost of debt e.g. 5.6%	x	% debt e.g. 35%			
Cost of equity (risk free + risk premium) e.g. 13.5%	x	% equity e.g. 65%	=	WACC 10.7%	

*Assumptions: Constant EBIT
Operating Capital Expenditure = Depreciation
Taxable Income = Accounting Income
No increase in working capital.

Reviewing the last decade, we would also discover that a lot of service industries have had attractive returns significantly above their cost of funds. If we examined recent figures for some new high-technology or internet-based businesses, we might find unattractive returns. For these industries we would need to make a judgment about their future attractiveness over the next decade as their market grows significantly.

A simple categorisation of profitability can just be:

► Low (below average cost of funds)

► Medium (at or slightly above average cost of funds)

► High (obviously above average cost of funds).

An informative analysis to undertake for your industry is **value chain analysis**. A typical supply chain for an industry is shown in Figure 4.3 below. Simple value chain analysis requires understanding the average returns from each segment in the supply chain. You may then formulate future strategies in terms of forward or backward integration. For example, if your direct suppliers are achieving a significantly higher return than the rest of the chain, you should look at backward integration.

Figure 4.3 – Average % returns of a typical supply chain

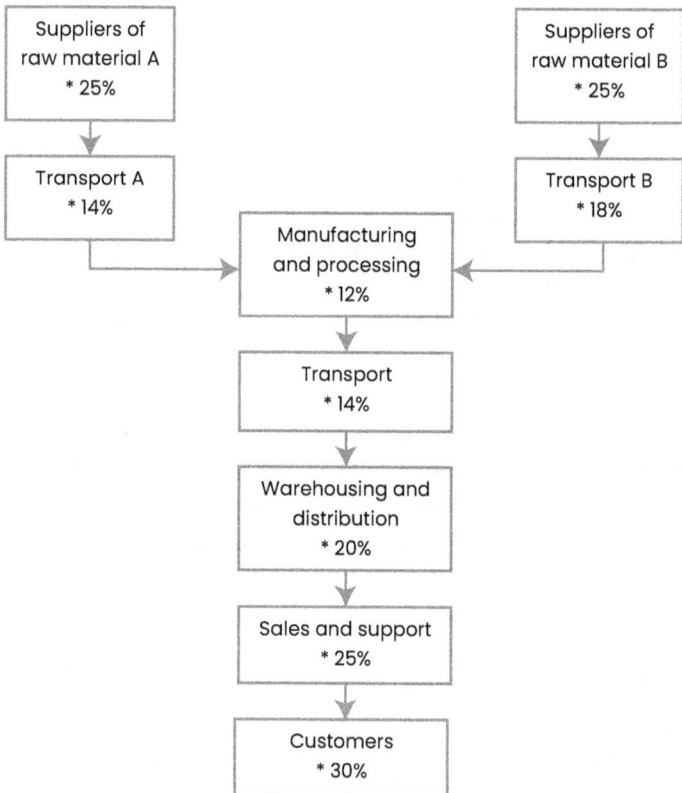

* = Average ROFE

Competitive structure

Understanding industry competitive structure is a fundamental part of strategic analysis. There are key structural features of industries that determine the strength of competitive forces and hence industry profitability.

There are three fundamental areas that influence the competitive structure of your industry. They relate to the level of aggression displayed by your existing competitors, the potential for new competitors and the influence up and down your supply chain. Figure 4.4 illustrates the forces driving industry competition.

Figure 4.4 - Forces driving industry competition

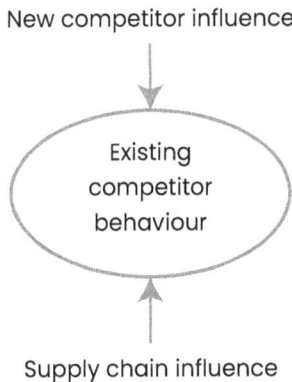

New competitor influence

Existing competitor behaviour

Supply chain influence

I will now explain these three competitive forces in more detail.

New competitor influence

New entrants to an industry, either with the same product or a substitute technology, can have the effect of lowering prices and increasing average costs, therefore reducing profitability. The threat of entry is low if there are enough barriers to entry in place. It can be difficult for new competitors to enter if:

- You are a higher volume business with low costs.
- You have loyal customers who value your product range.
- It takes a large amount of capital to enter your industry.
- It costs your customers a lot of money to change suppliers.
- There is no easy channel for new competitors to get their product to market.
- There are government restrictions such as licensing.

Behaviour among existing competitors

Rivalry among competitors comes from perceived pressure or perceived opportunity. If rivalry is too intense, then all companies in the industry will be worse off in terms of profitability. Rivalry can be intense if:

- Competitors are about the same size.
- The industry is not growing.
- It is hard to exit the industry.
- Products are basically commodities.
- Competitors have high fixed costs.

The factors that determine the intensity of competitive rivalry do change over time. Once you understand the factors influencing rivalry in your industry you can ensure your strategies optimise your position. For example, you might make it harder for your customers to leave through technology or you might direct your business towards the growing segments of the market.

Supply chain influence

Customers have an impact on industry profitability by pushing for lower prices and higher quality or more service. Customers have influence if:

► There is a small number of them relative to the sellers.

► The products are commodities.

► It is easy to change suppliers.

► They can backward integrate (supply themselves).

Suppliers have an impact on industry profitability by pushing for higher prices or lower quality of goods and services. Suppliers have influence if:

► There is a small number of them relative to the customers.

► There are no substitute products.

► The industry is not an important customer base.

► Their product is vital to your business.

► It is hard to change suppliers.

► They can forward integrate (be their own customer).

Again, supplier influence can change over time with industry structure and technology and it is an important area of strategy formulation.

This section on competitive structure has identified many factors that can potentially influence industry competition. Not all factors will be relevant in any one industry. For your industry it could be that only a few factors are relevant. What I have provided for you here is a sensible framework to help you identify structural features determining the nature of competition in your industry.

A final overview of competitive structure can allow you to broadly categorise it as:

► Weak
► Medium
► Strong.

The weak competitive environment would have a low rating on the three areas of competitive influence. The strong competitive environment would have a high rating on most areas.

No industry will be void of competitive forces but, obviously, the weaker the competitive environment the more attractive the industry.

Market diversity

The more diverse the range of market segments covered by your industry's products, the more attractive your industry is. An industry is open to significant risk if its fate rests with a single market segment. The attractiveness of market diversity comes from the fact that different segments will have different growth rates and different demand cycles. This can smooth out the demand for products and allow a more efficient use of resources.

Figure 4.5 gives a simple example of how market segment demand can smooth out total demand. Consider a building material product that sells into three market segments: domestic construction, commercial construction and rural. Although the segments fluctuate considerably, the total demand remains reasonably stable.

Figure 4.5 – Market segment demand

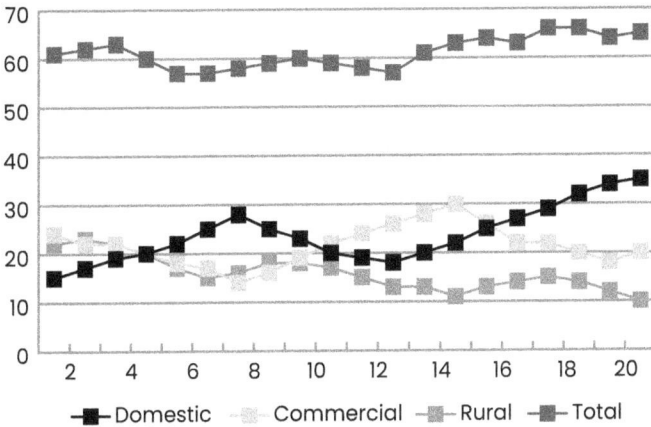

Another example would be an accounting firm that provides services into a number of market segments such as registered clubs, pharmacists, medical practitioners and family general stores. Again, the total demand is more likely to be stable compared to the demand from individual segments.

For this factor we can apply a simple rating of:

► Low (less than 3 segments)

► Medium (3 to 5 segments)

► High (greater than 5 segments).

Cyclicability

Cyclicability, to some extent, is related to market diversity. The more extreme the cyclical nature of demand for an industry's products, the less attractive the industry is. The charts in Figure 4.6 indicate some typical examples of cyclical demand for products.

The cyclical nature of demand can make it very difficult to organise resources.

Figure 4.6 – Typical examples of cyclical demand

Restaurant example of weekly demand

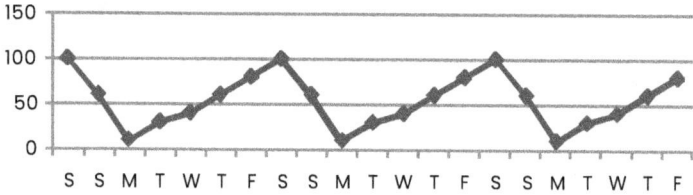

Ski hire example of annual demand

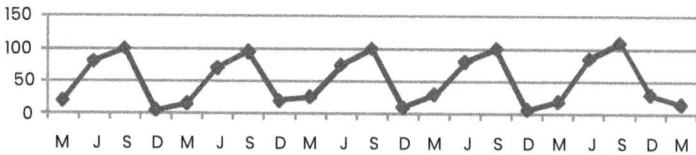

Domestic building material example of 4-year demand cycle

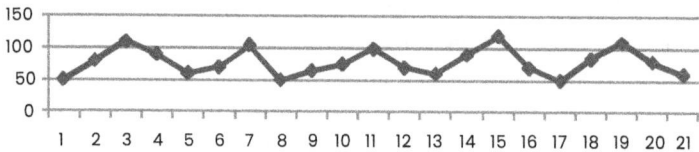

This area can have a simple rating of:

- Low (no obvious cycles)
- Medium (minor smooth cycles)
- High (obvious repetitive cycles).

Community risk

The severity of laws and demands on industry with respect to occupational health and safety (OH&S) and environmental compliance will only become harsher over the next few years. Industries are obviously more attractive if they have little risk in this area.

Manufacturing industries are particularly at risk from OH&S and environmental factors. Excellent systems and expertise of staff can overcome these risks and, in some industries, a particular company with skills in this area can have a competitive advantage. For a new entrant, the need for these systems and skills can be a significant barrier to entry. This characteristic of industry attractiveness can have a simple rating of:

- Low (very low risk of a major incident)
- Medium (some risk of a major incident)
- High (risk of a major incident every few years).

Specific industry overview

Now it is time to use all the discussion points above about industry attractiveness to gain an overview of a particular industry. Table 4.2 gives a notional industry attractiveness summary for a business. It lists the factors for industry attractiveness. It then gives a rating for a notional industry. It also gives the ideal attractiveness rating for each factor. From this table you can get a balanced view of the attractiveness of the industry. Although it doesn't reach the ideal on every factor the example industry is generally on the attractive side.

Table 4.2 – Industry attractiveness – notional services industry

Attractiveness factor	Industry rating	Ideal rating	Comment
Growth (Does the industry growth potential exceed GDP growth?)	High	High	Ageing population, complex advice
Size (Is there enough size in the industry for diversity of competition?)	Above target	Above target	There is a wide range of providers
Profitability (Do the average returns on all products exceed the average cost of funds?)	Medium	High	Similar firms make reasonable but not high returns, niche potential
Competitive structure (Is the industry highly competitive?)	Strong	Weak	Major competitor rivalry Strong customer influence Need reputation advantage
Market diversity (Are there a lot of market segments that spread the risk?)	Medium	High	Operates in four market segments
Cyclicability (Are there extreme cycles in the industry?)	Medium	Low	Minor cycles exist in the industry
Community risk (Are there major OH&S or environmental risks?)	Low	Low	No major risks
Key conclusions: The industry is moderately attractive but niche firms with unique characteristics could enjoy high returns.			

SWOT analysis

SWOT is an acronym for Strengths, Weaknesses, Opportunities and Threats. SWOT is now considered a standard tool for business analysis. If it is carried out by people with a good knowledge of your industry and your company, it does not take that long for this analysis to give you a valuable summary of your business.

The great value of this analysis is that it provides a clear framework for formulating future strategies. It forces you to take a candid look at your business. Strengths and weaknesses are part of your internal organisation. They are the areas that you control and can change with an internal focus. Opportunities and threats are fundamentally driven by outside forces. They need to be understood and your company needs to put actions in place to compensate or take advantage of the situation. As you plan based on your SWOT analysis you can formulate strategies to take advantage of the strengths and opportunities and to minimise the weaknesses and threats.

Tables 4.3 and 4.4 on the next pages are examples of a SWOT analysis for a manufacturing company and a management services company.

To get the best value from a SWOT analysis it is worthwhile to have a group session with valued management, employees and, if possible, some outside associates, customers or suppliers who understand your business.

Table 4.3 – SWOT analysis table
– manufacturing company

Strengths	Weaknesses
• Vertical integration • Integrated product offer • Wide range of products • Wide geographic spread • Established export business • Strong skill base • Good assets • Size and market share • Proven ability to improve	• Low service levels • Weak customer relations • High fixed cost base • Slow to respond to market • Management skills • Internally focused • Under utilising assets • Industrial relations issues • Disparate systems
Opportunities	**Threats**
• Improved planning systems • Customer service excellence • Lower working capital • Cost rationalisation • New business in service • Exploit competitor weaknesses • Environmentally positive products • New products development • New technology	• Irrational competitor pricing • Competitor speed • Supplier power • Cyclic behaviour of industry • Complacency in the upturn • Losing key people • Loss of access to resources • Competitive products • Shrinking global market

Table 4.4 – SWOT analysis table
– management services example

Strengths	Weaknesses
• Wide customer base • Good procedural systems • Good support software • Reputation for quality service • Excellent recruitment system • Some 'big client' contracts	• Low charge out percentage • Only well known in our state • Not enough partners in place • Still viewed as second tier company
Opportunities	**Threats**
• Wider range of integrated services • Selling modified services on the internet • Companies contracting out • Build business in other states	• Rationalisation of industry • Major systems failure • Key people leave • Key alliance lost • Key clients leave

Competitor analysis

As is the case with general industry analysis, competitor analysis can be a massive task. The level of information and the complexity of the task will vary from industry to industry.

Again, there is a wide range of sources that provide information, for example:

- ► Industry observers
- ► Your employees
- ► Service providers
- ► Customers
- ► Suppliers
- ► Published company information.

You should always take the opportunity to be a customer of your competitor and to include competitor questions in any of your customer surveys.

You should understand any special positions a competitor has with respect to the key competitive forces introduced in the competitive structure section on industry attractiveness.

You should attempt a SWOT analysis for each of your major competitors and this can give you a good insight to their future strategies.

It is also worth conducting an analysis of your competitors' cost structures and product offerings as represented in the sample competitor map in Figure 4.7.

The graph shows that the target company is somewhere in the middle for product differentiation and cost structure. It has some cost advantage but by far the most competitive company is company D. This helps to clarify your strategies with respect to different competitors.

Figure 4.7 - Sample competitor map

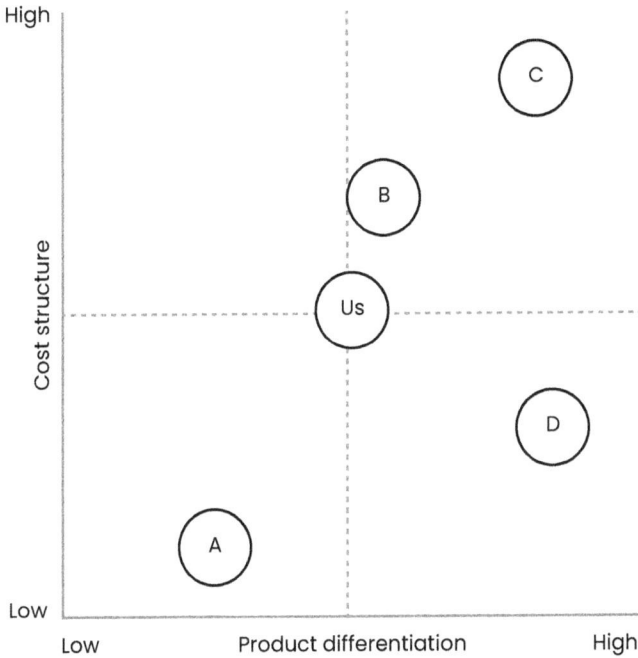

The sample competitor table overleaf, Table 4.5, is an example of some basic information you should have on the major competitors in your industry. As you can see, the target company has good performance, but company B is superior.

Table 4.5 – Sample competitor table

Competitor name (Top 5)	Us	B	C	D	E
Financials ($M)					
Assets	100	150	110	80	60
Sales	200	290	150	120	90
Profit	17	30	10	11	8
Cash flow	25	45	14	17	12
Gearing (%)	45	40	50	32	47
Customer survey (rating)					
Price	1	2	3	4	5
Quality	2	1	4	3	5
Delivery	3	2	4	1	5
Operating capacity (units/day)					
Product A	100	100	100	50	50
Product B	150	200	150	150	100
Product C	90	100	50	100	80
Product D	90	100	100	80	80
Market share (%)					
Product A	20	25	15	10	7
Product B	25	30	15	10	10
Product C	20	19	10	10	8
Product D	15	16	18	15	15
Overall rating	2	1	3	4	5

Customer analysis

To truly understand the forces that drive demand for your products, it is vital that you understand your customers and the contribution they make to your business. In many instances you need to understand your customers' customers.

Many companies find it difficult to segregate customer information because they have not set up the appropriate tracking in their financial systems. Most companies can track their revenue very well but have major trouble understanding their costs on a product and customer basis and yet this is vital for good decision making.

You should be able to identify revenue on a customer basis. You should also be able to segregate costs on a product and customer basis. This will allow you to have profitability information on a product and customer basis. It can be very useful, while undertaking a customer analysis, to review the supply chain influence discussion in the industry attractiveness section of this chapter. You should understand the bargaining power of each of your customers. Again, it can be valuable to perform a SWOT analysis on your major customers and understand how your business can add value to their future business strategies.

Table 4.6 overleaf is an example of some basic information you should have on your customers. You should know your key customers. You should understand the supply channel they use for their products. You should understand what percentage of your revenue they make up, but most importantly you should understand what percentage of your profit they deliver. As you can see, Customer A has the largest revenue but customers B and D are the ones to grow as their relative profit is higher.

Table 4.6 – Sample customer table

Customer name	A	B	C	D	E
Customer channel	X	X	Y	Y	X
Sales volume (units mil)					
Product A	16	18	13	10	6
Product B	10	14	5	6	5
Product C	20	8	11	9	11
Product D	22	15	10	8	11
Sales revenue ($M)					
Product A	42	38	25	19	12
Product B	28	45	13	18	14
Product C	45	18	22	20	21
Product D	35	19	12	9	13
Sales profit ($M)					
Product A	3	4	2	2	1
Product B	3	5	1	2	1
Product C	3	2	2	2	2
Product D	2	2	1	1	1
% of business revenue	15	12	8	6	6
% of business profit	10	15	6	8	5

Typical elements of a strategic plan

Putting a strategic plan in place, however detailed or streamlined, forces you to think through the position of your industry, your company within the industry and the strategic direction you need to take for future success. It is probably a fair statement that the process of planning is just as important as the plan itself. It is essential that you ask strategic questions about your industry and your company.

Although this chapter now gives you an outline of a typical strategic plan, the key message is that you need to be flexible enough to take advantage of a strategic opportunity – even if it is not specifically written in your strategic plan. If you take this attitude to planning, you will get maximum value from your work.

The basic elements of a strategic plan are:

- ► Summary of your industry and your company
- ► Environmental analysis summary and conclusion
- ► Industry attractiveness summary and conclusion
- ► SWOT analysis summary and conclusion
- ► Competitor analysis summary and conclusion
- ► Customer analysis summary and conclusion
- ► Identify underlying competitive advantage
- ► Long-term vision and values
- ► Key business strategies and measures.

The summary of your company and your strategic analysis tools is simply a logical lead in to explain why you have adopted a set of strategies. It basically consists of an identification of the key issues and key conclusions and a set of summary tables.

Let us now consider the other elements of a strategic plan.

Underlying competitive advantage

Underlying competitive advantage is the mix of your company's intellectual property, capabilities, skills and technologies that give you a sustainable advantage over your competitors. They can cluster to create competencies in an organisation. Those competencies that can lead your company to competitive advantage should be built on and protected. In order for your underlying competitive advantage to be sustainable it must:

► be relevant in a range of market segments;
► be viewed by customers as unique to your company; and
► be difficult for competitors to copy.

Understanding your potential for sustainable competitive advantage provides valuable input to strategic decision making. It provides a focus for the allocation of resources to leverage existing and build new advantage. It provides a new dimension to investment and divestment decisions. It highlights the opportunities for new markets, products and services.

The matrix in Figure 4.8 opposite can be useful in helping you sort through your identified capabilities, skills and technologies to ensure you have the right core competencies.

It is worth the time to identify your capabilities, skills and technologies and then to hone in on your developed or potential core competencies. This will provide a sound basis for developing your long-term vision and your key business strategies.

Listed below are a few competitive advantage examples:

1. **Operational excellence:** Supplying the right product to the right person at the right time and at the lowest cost.
2. **Product development:** Being the fastest at concept to market.
3. **Supply chain:** Controlling the supply chain from raw materials to end-use customers.
4. **Customer support:** Customers cannot survive without our systems.

Figure 4.8 – Skills development matrix

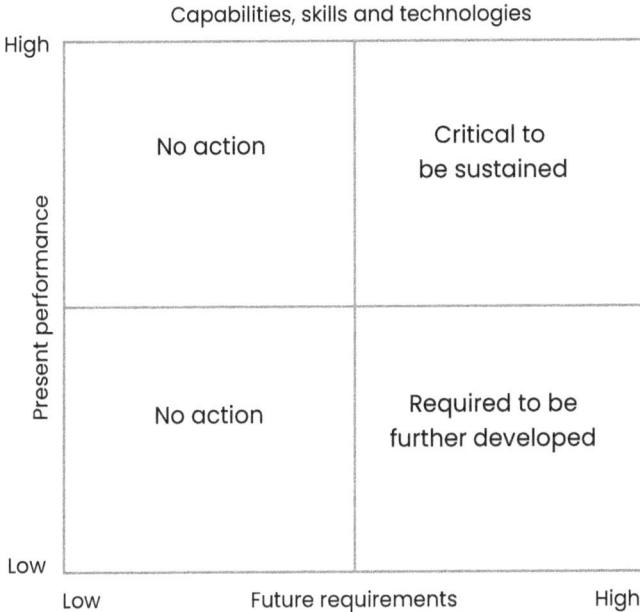

Capabilities, skills and technologies

	No action	Critical to be sustained
	No action	Required to be further developed

Present performance: High → Low

Future requirements: Low → High

Long-term vision and values

One of the most difficult challenges in management is developing a sense of vision and values. The following questions can help formulate your vision and values:

► Looking back on your history, what gives you the most pride?
► What could you do now that would make you proud?
► Ten years from now, what will you have done that would make you most proud?

A long-term **vision** is basically a statement of organisational ambition. That ambition creates energy in the organisation to achieve specific goals.

A vision should create a significant stretch for a company. This will encourage invention and making the most of a limited resource. With hindsight we can see that companies don't always get their visions right, but it really is the skill of developing the ambition that counts.

Whether your vision is grand or modest depends on your company's stage of development and its competitive threat. It is also worth noting that a vision means nothing if all your activities in your business do not back it up. A vision is stable over time. It should provide consistency to your short-term actions while leaving room for reinterpretation as new opportunities emerge.

Values are the organisational constants that dictate the way you conduct business. Values are about the personal behaviour of leaders and employees of the organisation.

Following are two example vision and value statements.

Example 1

Our Vision: To be the market leader in each of our chosen services.

Our Values:

- ► **Delivering quality to our customers:** We deliver quality work and our customers consider us to be their best supplier.
- ► **Trust:** We meet our promises.
- ► **Continuous improvement:** We challenge ourselves and continually strive to add value.

Example 2

Our Vision: To be the benchmark for our products.

Our Values:

- **Operational excellence:** We deliver the right product at the right time for the lowest possible cost.
- **Product innovation:** Our products are highly innovative and first to market.
- **People:** We provide sustainable employment and pathways to success for our people.
- **Safety:** Our goal is zero injuries and zero incidents.

Key business strategies and measures

Key **business strategies** are the central, integrated concepts of how the company will achieve its long-term vision. Your strategies should be based on the development and maintenance of sustainable competitive advantage. Your few key strategies should be simple, straightforward and easy to communicate within the organisation.

As is the case with vision, your key strategies should provide consistency to your short-term actions while leaving room for reinterpretation as new opportunities emerge.

Tables 4.7 and 4.8 give simple examples of a vision and the key strategies for a manufacturing and a services company. The examples enable more detailed business plans to be created to move the organisations along the path towards the vision and key strategies.

It is worth repeating that your vision and key strategies should provide direction for your shorter-term business plans while leaving room for reinterpretation as new opportunities emerge.

Let's look at the manufacturing example (Table 4.7). An analysis of the vision and the desired position columns in the key strategies example table highlight the potential key **long-term measures** for this manufacturing business. They would be:

► Customer survey comparisons with best supplier

► Delivery capability versus that of competitors

► Customer survey comparisons on product development

► Percentage of resource that is long-term access.

Table 4.7 – Manufacturing company example

Vision: To be our customers' best supplier

Key Business Strategies		
Competitive advantage	**Key strategy**	**Desired position**
1. Operational excellence	Integrate our well established production planning and sales systems	Our capability to deliver is half the time of our nearest competitor
2. Product development	Refine our existing product development system to half our concept to market time	Our customers see us as the market leader
3. Resource management	Develop a model of our resource availability and establish long-term contracts	We have a clear map of our resource availability and unique long-term access

Table 4.8 – Service company example

Vision: To be the first-choice logistics services company

Key Business Strategies		
Competitive advantage	Key strategy	Desired position
1. Supply chain management	Model whole supply chain for major customers	Flow from raw material to customer is optimised Our system is the best
2. Customer support	Develop linked IT systems in customers' premises	Customers need our systems to manage their business

The value of strategic analysis and planning

The value of strategic analysis and planning is that it forces you to understand your industry and your company's position within that industry. The very act forces you to think of the strategic possibilities, to identify your core competencies and to give your business strategic direction. The strategic direction gives you focus in these ever-changing times and allows you to develop meaningful short-term plans and performance measures.

Below I have given you an example strategic analysis and plan of a fictitious company, Jones Wall Systems.

Strategic analysis and plan example

Company background

Jones Wall Systems is a private family company that was established 30 years ago by William Jones. William is now the Non-Executive Chairman of the company and his son Brad Jones is the Managing Director.

The company has developed a pre-fabricated wall system that is delivered to site in manageable components then assembled on site by semi-skilled people.

The company has a history of providing good quality work and wall system innovation. It has consistently grown at a rate of 5% to 10 % per year over the last decade and is well established in its home state.

Over the last five years, the company has changed its product range to concentrate more on sustainable, energy-efficient wall systems and this has positioned it well for future growth.

The following pages give a strategic overview of the company and establish a strategic direction to be followed. This will be supported by a detailed three-year business plan.

1. Environmental analysis

External factor	Probability	Impact on business
Continued restrictions on house design to improve energy usage	High	Greater need for low-cost wall systems with excellent thermals
Reduced number of qualified building tradesmen	High	Greater need for manufactured wall systems
International residential building code	High	Good global opportunities
Wall system with similar features developed	Medium	Lose significant commercial advantage but still first in market
IP leaks out	Low/medium	Time and value leakage
Key component banned	Low	Big set back

Key conclusions: The general external trends support a cost competitive, easy-to-use wall system with good thermal characteristics, but we need first-mover advantage.

2. Industry attractiveness

Industry definition: Wall systems for residential and commercial use

Attractiveness factor	Industry rating	Ideal rating	Comment
Growth (Does the industry growth potential exceed GDP growth?)	Med/High	High	General construction matches GDP Energy efficient demand increasing
Size (Is there enough size in the industry for diversity of competition?)	Above target	Above target	There is a wide range of competition
Profitability (Do the average returns on wall products exceed the average cost of funds?)	Medium	High	Similar firms make reasonable but not high returns, niche potential
Competitive structure (Is the industry highly competitive?)	Strong	Weak	Major competitor rivalry Strong customer influence Need product and reputation advantage
Market diversity (Are there a lot of market segments that spread the risk?)	Medium	High	Operates in four market segments
Cyclicability (Are there extreme cycles in the industry?)	Medium	Low	Minor cycles exist in the industry
Community risk (Are there major OH&S or environmental risks?)	Low	Low	Manufacturing process relatively safe Product ingredients don't have major OH&S issues

Key conclusions: The industry is moderately attractive but niche firms with unique characteristics could enjoy high returns.

3. SWOT analysis

Strengths	Weaknesses
• Potentially unique combination of product properties • Less weather dependent • Competitive cost potential • Good delivery performance • Need for skilled labour reduced • Light weight benefits – OH&S, time, transport • Cleaner construction process • Strong reputation • Own IP	• First factory not optimised • Inexperienced manufacturer • Low volume producer • Only in one state • Process too manual • Lack of buyer power • Rely on transport company
Opportunities	**Threats**
• Scrutiny of building design • Unique building conditions in other states and countries • Government grants • Shortage of tradesmen • Environmental benefits • Other building products	• Rival product developed • Big manufacturers lock us out • Customers slow to accept • Poor product accreditation • Supply problems • Not being able to meet demand • Warranting • Incorrect installation • Under-resourced marketing

Key conclusions: Jones Wall Systems have great potential, but their large-scale commercial viability needs to be proven.

4. Competitor analysis

Competitor name (Top 5 – Eastern states)	Jones Wall Systems	B	C	D	E
Financials ($M)					
Assets	100	150	110	80	60
Sales	200	290	150	120	90
Profit	17	30	10	11	8
Cash flow	25	45	14	17	12
Gearing (%)	33	40	50	32	47
Customer survey (rating)					
Price	1	2	3	4	5
Quality	2	1	4	3	5
Delivery	3	2	4	1	5
Operating capacity (sq metres/day)					
Product A	100	100	100	50	50
Product B	150	200	150	150	100
Product C	90	100	50	100	80
Product D	90	100	100	80	80
Market share (%)					
Product A	20	25	15	10	7
Product B	25	30	15	10	10
Product C	20	19	10	10	8
Product D	15	16	18	15	15
Overall rating	2	1	3	4	5

Key conclusions: Our performance is good, but company B is superior.

5. Customer analysis

Customer name	A	B	C	D	E
Customer channel	X	X	Y	Y	X
Sales volume (sq metres/mil)					
Product A	16	18	13	10	6
Product B	10	14	5	6	5
Product C	20	8	11	9	11
Product D	22	15	10	8	11
Sales revenue ($M)					
Product A	42	38	25	19	12
Product B	28	45	13	18	14
Product C	45	18	22	20	21
Product D	35	19	12	9	13
Sales profit ($M)					
Product A	3	4	2	2	1
Product B	3	5	1	2	1
Product C	3	2	2	2	2
Product D	2	2	1	1	1
% of business revenue	15	12	8	6	6
% of business profit	10	15	6	8	5

Key conclusions: Customer A has the largest revenue, but customers B and D will grow as their relative profit is higher.

6. Underlying competitive advantage

Operational excellence: Supplying the right product to the right person at the right time and at the lowest cost.

Product development: Being the fastest at concept to market.

7. Our vision and values

Our Vision: To be the benchmark for wall systems.

Our Values:

► **Operational excellence:** We deliver the right product at the right time for the lowest possible cost.

► **Product innovation:** Our products are highly innovative and first to market.

► **People:** We provide sustainable employment and pathways to success for our people.

► **Safety:** Our goal is zero injuries and zero incidents.

8. Key strategies and measures

Jones Wall Systems Key Business Strategies		
Competitive advantage	**Key strategy**	**Desired position**
1. Operational excellence	Integrate our well established production planning and sales systems	Our capability to deliver is half the time of our nearest competitor
2. Product development	Refine our existing product development system to half our concept to market time	Our customers see us as the market leader

Scenario analysis and business modelling

Although your assumptions for your strategic plan and detailed business plans are obviously your view of what is most probable, understanding the implications of other scenarios is an extremely valuable exercise. Scenario analysis falls into two categories.

External scenario analysis

The first is **external scenario analysis**. This involves constructing alternative sets of likely conditions relating to the general external environment and your industry environment. The environmental analysis tool explained earlier in this chapter will help you create alternative conditions.

External scenario planning embraces uncertainty and devises a range of views of an uncertain future. Once you have defined a range of possible future scenarios you can determine the key strategies that are relevant to each scenario. You will find that some strategies will be common across all scenarios while others are only relevant to one or a few. Undertaking this type of analysis will make you more able to realign your strategies should external circumstances significantly change. In developing your strategic plan, you are simply taking the most likely external scenario as your base.

Internal scenario analysis

The second category of scenario analysis is **internal scenario analysis**. This assumes a particular external scenario is in place and that you are testing alternative business strategies to assess their impact. In order to measure the estimated value of different strategies you need to develop a business model.

A **business model** is a basic financial model of your business. It effectively projects what will happen to your profits, capital investment and cash flow over the next 5 to 10 years.

Table 4.9 below shows the output of a simple business model of future cash flow. Once the cash flows are determined, the net present value (NPV) of that model can be calculated. This gives you the present value of the future cash flows of the business and allows you to compare one alternative with another.

Table 4.9 – Sample business cash flow model

	Year						
	1	2	3	4	5	6	7
Inflows ($M)							
Revenue	15	16	18	22	25	29	33
Interest received	1	1	1	2	2	3	3
Total inflows	**16**	**17**	**19**	**24**	**27**	**32**	**36**
Outflows ($M)							
Cash operating costs	6	6	7	8	8	9	9
Equipment leases	2	2	2	2	2	2	2
Capital expenditure	2	2	3	4	4	5	5
Interest payments	2	2	2	3	3	3	3
Tax payments	2	2	3	3	4	5	6
Total outflows	**14**	**14**	**17**	**20**	**21**	**24**	**25**
Cash flow	**2**	**3**	**2**	**4**	**6**	**8**	**11**
NPV 38*							

* @ discount rate 10%

To get a thorough understanding of NPV you need to consult with finance experts. The following text is a simple explanation of NPV.

Net present value

The NPV of a business scenario is found by discounting the future after-tax cash flows at a specific discount rate. The discount rate is simply the rate of return the business must generate to justify raising funds.

Where there is perfect certainty about the outcome of the business venture, the risk-free rate, such as the current yield on government long-term securities, is an appropriate discount rate. However, as is generally the case where risk is involved, the discount rate would be the risk-free rate plus a risk premium. Many companies use their weighted average cost of capital (WACC) as their discount rate. I put this formula in for completeness below. You would obviously discuss the valuation of your business scenario with your financial adviser.

The formula for NPV is:

$$ NPV = \sum_{t=1}^{n} \frac{C_t}{(1+k)^t} $$

where: $\displaystyle\sum_{t=1}^{n}$ = sum the terms from year t=1 up to year t=n

n = the number of years the business model is over

k = the discount factor (e.g. 0.1= 10%)

C_t = the after-tax cash flow generated by the business in year t

C_n = the after-tax cash flow in the last year plus an estimate of the terminal value of the business*

*a simple estimate is cash flow x 8 (assumes a 12.5% discounted NPV)

Business option value analysis

Once you have calculated the NPVs and the average returns for your particular business scenario, you can place them on the graph below to see which scenario adds the greatest value. The greatest value will be added by those scenarios in the top right-hand corner. These scenarios will have the highest difference between their market value (NPV) and their book value and the greatest gap between their return on capital and cost of capital.

Figure 4.9 – Value analysis

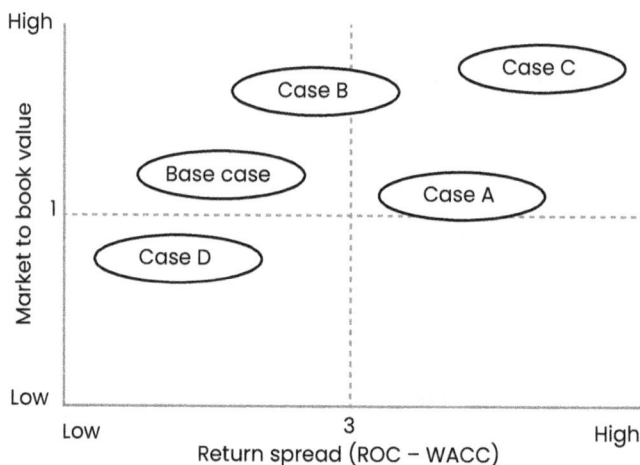

The simple scenarios in Figure 4.9 have used the same discount factor. If you have concerns about the relative risk of a particular scenario, then you should add a risk premium to the discount factor for that scenario. This will allow for your risk concerns in the value estimates of different options. As you can see, if the risk is manageable, then business option C is worth striving for. Remember risk and reward are always related.

Case Study – Clarity Pharmaceuticals

Clarity Pharmaceuticals was formed in 2010 by Dr Matt Harris and Tony Romagnino and, together with Dr Alan Taylor, they have grown this Australian company to a stage that it now has significant global potential.

Clarity Pharmaceuticals is a personalised medicine company focused on the treatment of serious disease. The company is a leader in innovative radiopharmaceuticals, developing targeted therapies for the treatment of cancer and other serious diseases in adults and children.

Clarity utilises its strong imaging capability and proprietary technology to develop novel radiopharmaceuticals. Clarity is expanding its program to tap into new markets that can be better served with their technology.

Below is the Clarity story in Matt Harris's own words.

Idea to commercial venture

The patents for Clarity's intellectual property (IP) position were found in 2008 by Dr Matt Harris and Tony Romagnino, who at the time were running TM Ventures (TMV). TMV had a business model to find great IP and build start-ups, so Matt and Tony found themselves scouting for IP at the Australian Nuclear Science and Technology Organisation (ANSTO) and the University of Melbourne (UoM). Matt recognised the first patent at ANSTO because of his background in Nuclear Medicine 15 years earlier and understood the technology and its potential applications. He then noticed similar work being done at UoM and pieced together that the patents overlapped. Both patent families were sitting there motionless (post GFC) in the technology transfer offices of their respective institutions and were therefore available for licensing. TMV created a new company and licensed the patents into the virgin company with the aid of Rosanne Robinson from ANSTO and Sean Lumb from UoM, the company's founding directors.

Clarity was conceived by the convergence of multiple factors. The entrepreneurial endeavours of TMV and desire to create a start-up just after the GFC were timed well with the availability of the patents for licensing and willingness of the institutions to license the IP into a new start-up.

In addition, Matt and Sean had the knowledge and background to recognise and believe that the technology was the foundation of a pharmaceutical company. Combined with the business acumen of Tony and Rosanne, it led to the development of a business plan that made sense and was drafted well for general investors to read.

Relentless willpower to try and pull the patents out of the respective institutions was needed, given it took 18 months to achieve. The founding inventors of the IP, Professor Suzanne Smith and Professor Paul Donnelly, were also very supportive of the start-up concept and willing to provide their research laboratories as a resource to further develop the technology.

Angel investors

Once the company was created and licences to the IP were secured, it was then on Matt and Tony's shoulders to find start-up capital. This is where a connection to Newcastle allowed them in the door at Hunter Angels, where Eileen Doyle was a member. Hunter Angels had never done a biotechnology investment and arguably had very little expertise in biotechnology. But what they could assess was the business plan and the people. They conducted their due diligence and were able to reach a decision to be in the first set of eight investors in Clarity – a gutsy move.

As a group, Hunter Angels would meet with Matt and provide advice on the early direction of the company. When Clarity started to generate revenue, the questions and advice on profit margins by the Angels helped guide the development of that business unit. Their patience and respect for the development of each new business unit at the time best suited to the company was appreciated by the founders. Their networks and introduction to various people and groups in Newcastle were also important. Clarity has required multiple rounds of investment and the Hunter Angels have invested in a number of rounds as well as a number of the Angels investing on their own. This has helped the company with new investors coming in who gain confidence in their high-risk investment through the supportive base of original investors.

Transition from start-up to promising pharmaceutical company

After two rounds of investment totalling approximately $1 million (AUD), which enabled two to three years of early development, the company needed to grow and transition from a start-up with promising tech to a company offering services and building products.

Matt and Tony were able to recruit a very successful investment banker to the company as Executive Chairman, Dr Alan Taylor. Alan brought extensive experience in capital markets, mergers and acquisitions and general corporate advisory as well as a deeper network of investors. Alan's background, which is rare in Australia and was very complementary for Clarity, was a combination of science and many years of investment banking, which included being involved in a number of the largest ever medical device transactions in Australia.

The securing of the initial IP, which was funded by angel investment, was essential in attracting a seasoned person in biotechnology like Alan to help lead the company as the company's Executive Chairman. In the five years following up to 2018, Alan and Matt have complemented each other's skills and experience to set and achieve strategic objectives and build an outstanding team of professionals to execute on delivering clinical trials to better treat children and adults with cancer.

With the help of Matt and the team, Alan structured a number of capital raisings for Clarity and the company was able to raise an additional $7 million in equity as well as approximately $8 million in grants and other non-dilutive funding.

Alan and Matt used this capital to translate the technology into a number of products, including Clarity's lead product SARTATE™, an oncology drug for the treatment of a range of cancers in children and adults.

Clarity has successfully built an international network of thought leaders in the field to develop its products and it has facilitated a collaborative model, which enabled the company to access world leading advisers, build an extensive IP position and utilise best-in-class facilities to execute on its product development initiatives.

With all of these important steps for a company translating good Australian science, Clarity now finds itself in the enviable position of being a clinical stage biotechnology company developing efficacious products for the treatment of a number of serious cancers in children and adults, supported by a world class team of staff and advisers. At the time of writing this piece, Clarity was in a number of strategic discussions around larger capital raisings and other transaction opportunities with a range of companies around the world.

Dr Matt Harris, 2018, Founder and Managing Director, Clarity Pharmaceuticals

CHAPTER 5
THE BUSINESS PLANNING TOOLKIT

Business plans and budgets are vital for setting clear, short-term direction and measurable targets. Although the strategic plan provides the ambition for a company, preparing one would only be an academic exercise if there were not a business plan and budget to back it up.

Your **business plan** is a description of how your vision and long-term strategies will be achieved over the next couple of years. It provides a set of shorter-term measures of performance.

Your **budget** provides further financial detail for the next year. It projects the detail behind the next year's profit, capital requirements and cash flow.

Essential elements of good business plans

There is a lot of jargon used in this area and where possible it is best to avoid it. The value of business planning comes from the involvement in the process and the clear establishment of short-term targets and activities.

The essential elements of good business plans are:

- Simple directions and strategies
- A standard format to aid deployment

► A simple process with a clear timetable

► Good participation for surfacing of issues

► Logical links between different levels of the organisation.

Let's elaborate on each of these areas.

Keep directions and strategies simple

Your statement of future direction and your strategies should be simple and easily able to be remembered. A summary of your business plan direction should fit on a couple of pages and it should be laid out in such a way that it is straightforward to explain. The next section on standard format will show how this can be done.

Standard format to aid deployment

A simple, standard format should be used in all sections of the company (e.g. at corporate level, business unit level and section level). The one-page business plan tool given in Figure 5.1 shows a typical business plan format that I have used on a number of occasions.

With reference to Figure 5.1, the mission statement is a statement of where your company wants to be over the next two to three years. It should include your products, your market and the position you want to hold in that market.

Figure 5.1 – The one-page business plan

"What we want to be"

```
┌──────────────┐
│  Mission     │        "Key measures of success"
└──────┬───────┘
       │         ┌──────────────────┐
       └────────▶│    Measures      │
       │         └──────────────────┘
       ▼
```

"How we get there"

```
┌──────────────┐
│  Strategies  │
└──┬────┬───┬──┘
   ▼    ▼   ▼
```

"How we achieve strategies"

```
┌──────────────┐
│  Activities  │
└──────┬───────┘
       ▼
```

A simple example of a mission statement would be:

To be the Leading Supplier of Breakfast Products in Australia

The **key measures** should be focused around stakeholder value. They should reflect contribution to:

► Shareholder value
► Customer value
► Supplier value
► Employee value
► Community value
► Organisation value.

Key measures should have some stretch but be achievable.

The **strategies** are the few, principal ways the mission will be achieved. They should state which broad areas will be addressed to progress the longer-term, key business strategies in the strategic plan.

The **activities** are the specific broad actions that will support the strategies.

The detailed **action plans** support the activities and will be discussed later in the chapter.

Simple process with a clear timetable

A simple process should be used to pull the business plan together. For example, a basic, strategic analysis and plan should be prepared, presented and discussed with your key management team. The business plan should then be developed by that group to provide detailed support to the strategic plan. The business planning process should be undertaken or reviewed at the same time each year, prior to preparing the detailed budget for the next year.

Good participation for surfacing of issues

As described above, it is worth involving your key teams of people at corporate or business unit level in your business planning. The very discussion of the strategic analysis and plan, and the development of the business plan across your organisation, creates an environment where significant issues can be raised, discussed and worked through. A genuine engagement of your people/teams promotes participation, discussion and debate on options at both the strategic and tactical levels.

Logical link established between the different levels of the organisation

When a business plan is being prepared at the corporate level, the business unit level and the section level, then it is vital that there is a logical link between the plans. The missions at the lower levels should support the mission at the next level up. The measures and strategies at the lower levels should be consistent with those at the next level up. This will ensure all areas of the company are working together. This requires engagement with and dialogue between the levels to ensure a coherent business plan and one that all levels have ownership of.

Sample company business plans

To give you an idea of what a completed business plan looks like, I have put together sample business plans for a building materials company and a professional services company. This is the best way to explain what should be in each section of the plan. On the first page of the plan you will find an example mission, key measures and strategies. The next page gives example activities.

Sample manufacturing company's business plan (typically 3 years)

We want to be ...

> An internationally competitive equipment supplier to our domestic and selected export markets

The key measures of our success will be ...

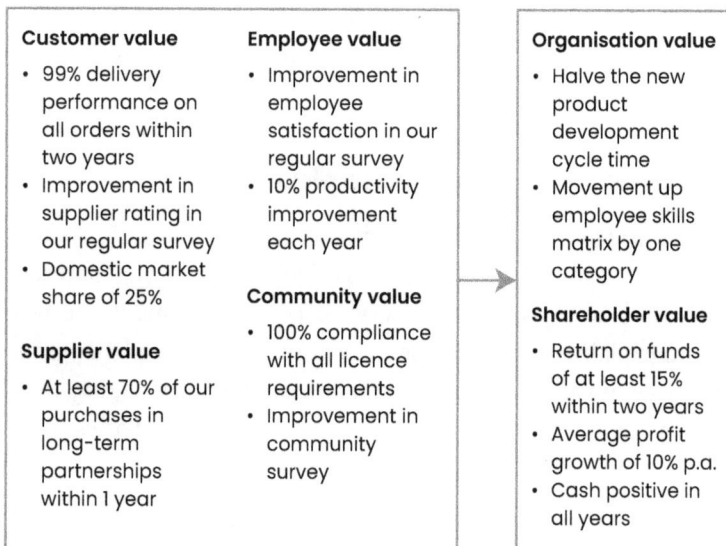

Customer value

- 99% delivery performance on all orders within two years
- Improvement in supplier rating in our regular survey
- Domestic market share of 25%

Supplier value

- At least 70% of our purchases in long-term partnerships within 1 year

Employee value

- Improvement in employee satisfaction in our regular survey
- 10% productivity improvement each year

Community value

- 100% compliance with all licence requirements
- Improvement in community survey

Organisation value

- Halve the new product development cycle time
- Movement up employee skills matrix by one category

Shareholder value

- Return on funds of at least 15% within two years
- Average profit growth of 10% p.a.
- Cash positive in all years

We will achieve these outcomes by ...

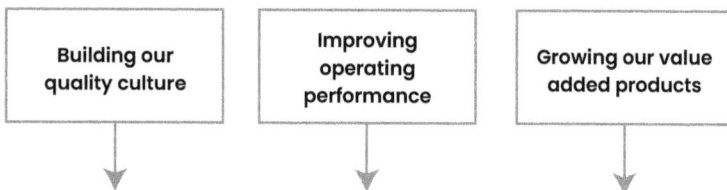

Building our quality culture	Improving operating performance	Growing our value added products

The Business Planning Toolkit

Through these key activities ...

• Process control measurement on all key factory variables in 18 months • All standard operating procedures reviewed in 12 months • Implement clean-up and improvement activities which meet community standards • Continue employee movement up the skills matrix	• Link our sales orders directly to the factories within 18 months • Introduce formal sales and operations planning meetings within six months • Outsource of product transport to reduce cost and improve delivery performance within 12 months • 25% reduction in inventory within 12 months	• Identify and develop further income-generating activities from our existing assets • Introduce a tailored new product development program within six months • Double our research and development funding for product development within 12 months

↓ ↓ ↓

Action plans

Sample service company's business plan
(typically 3 years)

We want to be ...

Well known in our region as an innovative professional firm that partners with our target customer base

The key measures of our success will be ...

- Turnover of $5m within 1 year
- Turnover of $15m within 3 years
- At least 30 clients with a fee base > $300,000 within 3 years
- At least 100 clients with a fee base > $40,000 within 3 years
- Staff avoidable turnover rates of < 5%
- At least 4 strategic professional partners in place within 3 years
- All major support systems in place within 1 year

We will achieve these outcomes by ...

Developing effective enabling systems	Building on our established professional approach	Growing our target customer base

Through these key activities ...

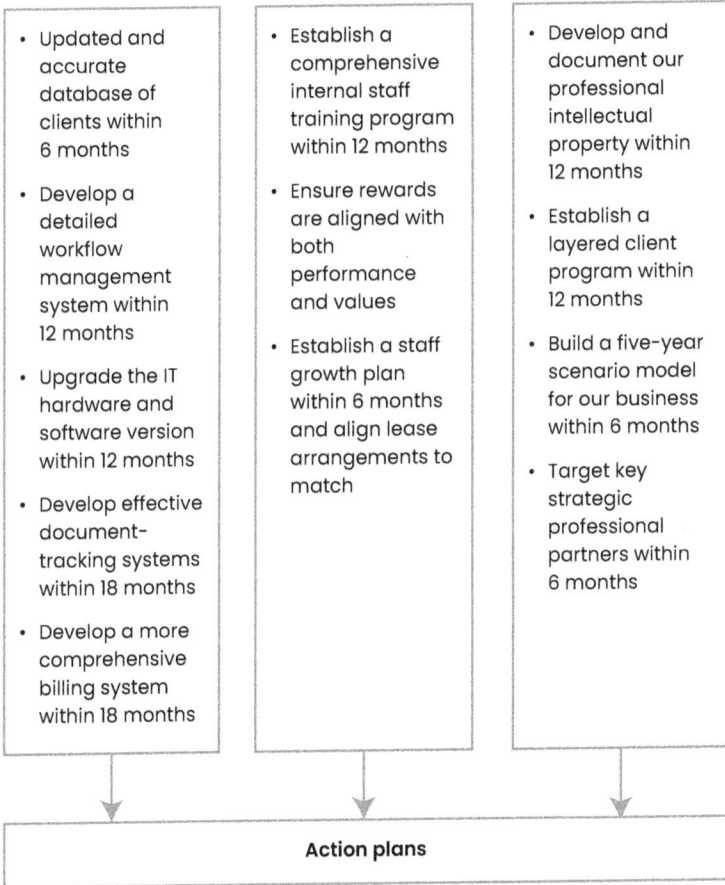

• Updated and accurate database of clients within 6 months • Develop a detailed workflow management system within 12 months • Upgrade the IT hardware and software version within 12 months • Develop effective document-tracking systems within 18 months • Develop a more comprehensive billing system within 18 months	• Establish a comprehensive internal staff training program within 12 months • Ensure rewards are aligned with both performance and values • Establish a staff growth plan within 6 months and align lease arrangements to match	• Develop and document our professional intellectual property within 12 months • Establish a layered client program within 12 months • Build a five-year scenario model for our business within 6 months • Target key strategic professional partners within 6 months

Action plans

Action planning

Action plans are the practical day-to-day link with your business plan direction. Achieving planned actions is the way that the organisation moves forward.

The action plans support the business plan strategies and broad activities. A sample action plan will appear later in this chapter. It will be linked to the sample business plan in chapter three.

Typical format

Action plans need to be specific. They need to have a clear time-frame and allocate personal responsibility. A very basic format for action plans should at least have the following headings:

- Broad activity
- Action
- Timing
- Person responsible.

The above headings will be enough to provide a link to the business plan's broad activity and provide a timeframe to meet the business plan's measures.

Personal planning

Personal plans are the final link between the business plan and the individual. They form a good basis for performance reviews at the end of the year.

Personal plans should reference the business plan strategies and the person's work team activities as an overview to provide context for their personal activities. Their plan should outline their job goals, KPIs and personal development goals. It should also identify the key steps to achieve their goals, the measures of success and, at a later stage in the review process, the outcomes.

Personal plans should be signed by the individual and their direct supervisor and reviewed by the person one-up from their direct supervisor. Performance against the personal plans should be reviewed at least quarterly with an annual formal review. The detail of the review process and corrective action will be discussed in chapter six.

The value of supporting plans

Depending on the nature and complexity of your company, a basic business plan might not provide enough specific direction for some areas of the business. This is where you might need to draft some detailed supporting plans. These are usually necessary for complex companies handling a range of products and with a high involvement in product development.

Supporting plans cover the same timeframe as the business plan and their analysis and actions are supportive of the business plan's direction. The format of any action plans is similar to that which we have just covered in this chapter.

Common supporting plans cover the following areas:

► Marketing and sales
► Projects and portfolios.

The next two chapters will discuss each one of these support plan toolkits and give an example of the best format to use. For those readers who have smaller companies, the next few chapters are still valuable for you to read. Although you might not have these detailed plans you may well include elements of them in your business planning toolkit.

The budget

The budget is the detailed financial summary of the first year of the business plan. It typically projects month-by-month targets. It usually has a profit and loss and cash flow emphasis. It could be broken up into profit or cost centres, which sum together to create the company's budget.

The budget must be viewed as a commitment by management. Future actual performance or forecasts of future performance should be measured against the budget.

Table 5.1 opposite is an example profit and loss budget for a manufacturing company. Table 5.2 is the cash flow statement (see page 106). This budget would obviously have detailed workings to back it up at a cost centre level.

Table 5.1 – Sample profit and loss budget

	Jul	Aug ...	May	Jun	Full year
Revenue ($ '000s)					
Volume product A	10	15	17	12	150
Revenue product A	100	150	170	120	1,500
Volume product B	22	25	30	25	280
Revenue product B	110	125	150	125	1,400
Volume product C	13	12	11	14	150
Revenue product C	234	216	198	252	2,700
Other revenue	50	50	50	50	600
Total revenue	**494**	**541**	**568**	**547**	**6,200**
Cost of goods sold					
Labour costs	90	105	110	105	1,200
Material costs	110	116	120	115	1,400
Energy costs	42	42	42	42	500
Freight costs	49	54	57	55	620
Other costs	32	32	32	32	380
Total costs of GS	**323**	**349**	**361**	**349**	**4,100**
Contribution	171	192	207	198	2,100
Overheads					
Marketing and sales	20	20	20	20	240
Warehouse	22	22	22	22	264
Administration	10	10	10	10	120
EBIT	**119**	**140**	**155**	**146**	**1,476**
Interest	10	10	10	10	120
Tax	43	50	56	53	528
Profit	**66**	**80**	**89**	**83**	**828**
Funds employed	**4,500**	**4,500**	**4,590**	**4,700**	**4,700**

Table 5.2 – Sample cash flow budget

	July	Aug ...	May	Jun	Full Year
Revenue ($ '000s)					
Product sales	444	491	518	497	5,600
Investment revenue	50	50	50	50	600
Total revenue	**494**	**541**	**568**	**547**	**6,200**
Cash costs					
Operating costs	299	332	351	336	3,796
Investment costs	5	5	5	5	60
Overhead costs	42	42	42	42	504
Total cash costs	**346**	**379**	**398**	**383**	**4,360**
Trading cash flow	**148**	**162**	**170**	**164**	**1,840**
Capital expenditure	**0**	**0**	**90**	**110**	**200**
Operating cash flow	**148**	**162**	**80**	**54**	**1,640**
Tax payments	**0**	**0**	**0**	**126**	**505**
After-tax cash flow	**148**	**162**	**80**	**(72)**	**1,135**

Finally, to see the key ratios in the budget, you can pull them out and include a summary table (see Table 5.3).

Table 5.3 – Sample ratio budget

	July	Aug ...	May	Jun	Full Year
EBIT/sales	24%	26%	27%	27%	24%
Overheads/sales	10.5%	9.6%	9.2%	9.5%	10.1%
ROFE	31%	37%	41%	37%	31%

Case Study – Rapid Phenotyping

Rapid Phenotyping is an Australian company, formed in 2016 by Antony Martin, Jamie Flynn and William Palmer.

Using in-house, custom algorithms, they have developed a new, high-throughput platform that is compatible with any liquid or solid material. They have streamlined the process of calibrating accurate spectral predictions and making routine compositional analysis of materials rapid, cost-effective and accurate.

So far, they have applied this technology to rapid compositional analysis and online monitoring of agricultural and food products, but the possibilities are limitless.

Below is the Rapid Phenotyping story in Antony Martin's own words

———————

Co-founder Jamie Flynn and I go back a long way. We have always had ideas and, since I can remember, we have sought to commercialise these ideas; from a casino at the primary school mini fete, to a woodworking business in high school, to a self-constructed mobile pizza oven and a record label signed band throughout university. It was during this time at university that Jamie and I met co-founder William Palmer.

We were each completing PhDs at the University of Newcastle, in vastly different fields of life science, but found that we were connected on our vision to improve the way laboratory research and testing is conducted. This first materialised when our PhD projects came to an end and we were left with a decision to move abroad for a post-doctoral research position, or to start something of our own.

Of course, we chose to start something of our own. We had two developed ideas at this point. However, the choice of which to pursue was made for us when we were given significant support from the Hunter Medical Research Institute, through a philanthropic donation, to construct a novel 3D imaging facility. This included a chemical processing setup, the construction of a 3D optical light-sheet microscope and a virtual biobank web platform for large-scale processing and display of important medical tissue samples in 3D.

We delivered the facility on time and on budget, partly due to the fact that we shared a part-time wage between the three of us, but quickly realised that, while this was a beneficial research facility, the commercial applications were limited. This project also gave us community exposure, experience delivering complex optical hardware products and big data handling software and it put us in contact with angel investors for the first time. We realised that angel investors were interested in our ideas and that if we were able to structure and validate our ideas into a commercial business, there was support available in many forms, from advice to active mentoring, to capital.

The company we are now operating, Rapid Phenotyping, initially began during this foray into the world of 3D imaging, as a means for earning some extra cash by massively increasing the efficiency at which scientists could conduct certain lab tests.

As I said, we were working at the Hunter Medical Research Institute, sharing a wage between three, and in the remainder of our time, looking to increase our income by conducting lab tests for researchers faster and cheaper than they could do themselves. This was successful, and it earned us a bit of cash to help pay the bills, but we quickly realised it was not scalable under the service model as we were physically required to process thousands of samples for customers.

At around this time we set on our journey of engaging the business community by setting up an advisory board and engaging some government grant programs. This led to engagement of Glenn Turner, our angel mentor and eventual angel investor from the Hunter Angels. Looking back, although he wouldn't come on board as an investor until a year later, he quickly became an invaluable mentor, guiding us through IP negotiations with universities, patenting processes, business models and customer validations, and he helped in gaining a government grant to support product development. Step-by-step, Glenn took us through the process of gathering information for what would turn out to be our pitch to angel investors.

I cannot understate the importance of engaging an early stage mentor with angel investment experience and networks before approaching angel investors for seed capital, unless you have previous experience doing so yourself. We were researchers with limited business experience and the mentorship we received, and continue to receive from our seed stage investors, has been the greatest crash course in business that anyone could dream of. It has allowed us to set up commercial processes and prepare the company as an investable business.

Within months of engaging the local business community and mentorship from angel investors, we were able to receive a substantial government grant as well as support from the University of Newcastle as a very early customer. This provided our first opportunity to transform our non-scalable service model into a hardware product and smartphone/web app that would allow global scale.

Hardware is hard, so software came first for us. Our first step away from the 100% service-based approach to lab testing was to implement our software platform that could take inputs from the old lab service system and automatically generate results for unlimited numbers of samples at the click of a button. This minimised the amount of work required by about 40% but did not replace the requirement for one of us to physically process samples.

We gained customers under this model and showed that they were willing to pay for the results. Next, we moved to a model that used an OEM hardware device that could perform limited testing but completed our platform. This was our first real minimum viable product (MVP) that removed 100% of the service aspect, although with limited capability. This MVP was deployed with partners and a small number of customers to generate feedback and allow us to perform beta testing and begin the process of incrementally improving the service. All of this information was also able to be constantly fed into product development of our flagship device.

Developing hardware for our flagship device has been difficult and expensive and, especially in our case, funding initial manufacturing runs of a high value product has been difficult. We landed on the only practical way forward, and that is pre-sales of hardware. It took us a little while (plus some positive prototype testing) to not be afraid to pre-sell something we did not yet have, but this seemed to be the only viable approach. Whether it be via online crowd-funding or simply getting out there and selling it, pre-sales are the best way to validate that the market is willing to pay and to fund manufacturing runs.

During this process we have also been sure to set up to scale – meaning that any process that wasn't able to exponentially scale had to be examined and re-engineered. For us, a critical element that was not scalable was the calibration of new lab tests that required a machine learning component with high sample inputs. We pivoted our business model to allow crowd sourcing of these samples and data from partners who are now not only exponentially increasing the input data into our system but opening up new channels to market for themselves and us through our marketplace model for online lab testing.

We received a $360,000 grant from AusIndustry under their Entrepreneurs Program and this was matched by consulting work, mostly from the University of Newcastle that were very supportive of us and also with family and director loans, and other projects including with CSIRO.

We very quickly gained a number of projects with the International Rice Research Institute (IRRI) in the Philippines, where we delivered 60,000 test results in the space of a few weeks. This would have otherwise been completely unachievable for them or would have taken years and millions of dollars. This was our first large project and it generated $30,000 in revenue. We also continued some other smaller projects in Australia. These projects were under the service model and we quickly pivoted to focus on hardware and software development after this. To do so we required capital and went to seed investors where we raised $880,000 to develop the most advanced handheld spectrometer on the market. This was recently also matched with a continuation of our Entrepreneurs Program grant providing a further $630,000 in funding.

The early funding also allowed, and required us, to build out a team which began with our incredible Chief Technology Officer Peter Tylee who has built a world-class artificial intelligence software platform, optical engineer Dr Rod Vance who has helped us generate more patentable material than we can afford to patent and turn our hardware into a reality. It has allowed us to conduct trials and customer interviews and to establish business processes including all the stuff you don't think about when you have a great idea: accounting processes, employment contracts, IP strategies, sales processes, customer agreements, etc. It also gave us the time required to work with our mentors to build evidence to support the key elements investors look at when assessing an early stage investment. All of this formed the basis of our pitch to seed stage investors.

In our seed round, we were lucky to only officially pitch with slides on two occasions. Most of the real pitches to investors were done unexpectedly over a coffee, a beer, in an office, or in a board meeting without slides. A number of follow-up meetings and demonstrations were then requested and performed in different locations, ranging from the 19th floor looking over the Sydney harbour bridge, to an investor's garage, to a wheat weigh bridge in the middle of nowhere. Once these seed stage investors were on board, they became the most valuable assets to our business. I am constantly astounded by how much work they do on our business behind the scenes and they are always calling me, Jamie and Will with valuable advice, contacts, offering to sit down with us to nut out a problem, and instructing us on how to navigate our way over our next hurdle, a Series A raise designed to get the company into US markets. Without early and consistent mentorship from angel investors we would not be where we are today.

We now have an MVP hardware product that has generated some sales, but it has mostly been used for beta testing with partners. More prominently, we have $100,000 in pre-sales of our hardware and $1.6m in the sales pipeline with >50% in the final stages of negotiation. Our flagship product is currently being manufactured with the first runs due in October. We are excited to get this product into labs from agricultural testing to petrochemical testing, to medical testing, where we can work with them as partners to build out huge in-field testing capabilities to service the agricultural market and make supply chains more transparent with trackable quality and contamination information. We have a big vision. Our angel investors keep our feet on the ground and make sure we focus our attention on the next sale and nailing one specific testing area before building toward the next.

Dr Antony Martin, 2018, Founder and CEO

CHAPTER 6
THE MARKETING TOOLKIT

Marketing and sales plans are useful for describing the different situation for each product or service and providing specific detailed direction for sales staff.

Elements of the marketing and sales plan

The marketing and sales plan for a particular offering should at least contain:

- A definition of the market
- Market size
- Competitor comparisons
- Marketing objective
- Supporting strategies
- Expenditure breakup
- A tactical plan.

Definition of market

The definition of market is a basic description of the offering and where it is used, for example:

We provide domestic external wall cladding products in sheet and plank form for use in new homes, renovations, extensions and some light commercial building applications;

Or:

We provide four-star accommodation and services to business and leisure customers in Australasia.

Market size

An estimate of the market size, region by region where relevant, is important to understand the scale of the market. This gives some realism to the size and scale of resources you will require, your likely market share and domestic and international targets.

Competitor comparisons

It is very important to understand your position with respect to your competitors in areas such as price, distribution, product quality, promotion and product service and support. It is also important to understand the priority of importance of these areas to the customer.

It is worth preparing a table listing the priority of importance, the product factor and your estimated rating for your own company and your major competitors. You will see an example of this later in the sample marketing and sales plan (starting on page 117). You should also have an estimate of the sales volume, market share and market share trend for your company and your major competitors.

Marketing objective

Your marketing objective is what you want to achieve in a marketing sense for your product over the life of the plan. It could be about market share, pricing, new product or service introduction or distribution channel changes.

A simple example of a marketing objective is:

To increase the domestic market share of product A to 18% at the expense of competitor Y.

Supporting strategies

The supporting strategies are a description of how you will achieve your marketing objective.

Your competitor comparisons indicate how you compare to your major competitors on particular areas such as product, price, promotion, distribution and service/support. Supporting strategies should also cover these areas.

For example, to support the marketing examples in the previous section, you could have the following supporting strategies:

Example supporting strategies

1. Wall cladding product

Product:	Differentiate range with unique new lines Improve product packaging
Price:	Position between competitor Y and X
Promotion:	Enhance online ordering: continue pull through by customer's customer
Distribution:	Increase number of distribution centres
Service/support:	Improve staff training and point of sale

2. Accommodation service

Product:	Refurbish rooms with a common theme
	Upgrade internet access and options
	Revitalise restaurant menus
Price:	Position total experience cost to be in top quartile but below competitor Y
Promotion:	Continue with targeted advertising
	Upgrade website
	Refresh loyalty scheme
Distribution:	Increase number of regions covered
Service/support:	Improve front office and housekeeping services

Expenditure breakup

Expenditure breakup should indicate your likely expenditure over the next year to help achieve the marketing and sales plan.

The expenditure breakup should cover areas such as market research, point of sale material, advertising and promotion and staff training. An example is given in Table 6.1 below. The nature of your industry will have a significant bearing on the level of expenditure required in the areas mentioned.

Table 6.1 Example expenditure breakup

Area of expenditure	Amount
Market research	$220K
Point of sale	$120K
Advertising and promotion	$500K
Sales staff training	$90K
Total	**$930K**

Tactical plan

The marketing and sales tactical plan is the next level down of detail to add specifics to the marketing objective and supporting strategies. For each strategy you need to define the specific tactics or actions, the planned results and the target finish date.

You will see an example of a tactical plan table later in the sample marketing and sales plan.

Sample marketing and sales plan

To give you an idea of what a completed marketing and sales plan looks like, I have put together a sample plan for a building materials product company. It is presented on the next few pages and is the best way to explain what should be in each section of the plan.

Sample plan

1. Definition of business

We provide external roof cladding products for use predominantly in the domestic residential market for new homes, renovations and extensions.

2. Marketing objective

To increase the market share of "Roofclad" from 12% to 15% at the expense of tiles and metal roofing.

3. Market size

The annual domestic residential market for roofing products for new homes, renovations and extensions is approximately $1.5 billion.

4. Competitor comparisons

Table 6.2 below is an example of some of the basic information you should have about your customers' preferences and how your competitors' performance relates to your performance.

Table 6.2 – Competitor table

Factor/priority to customer	Competition (10=best, rest relative)					
	Us	B	C	D	E	F
Price (3)	7	7	2	3	5	8
Distribution (2)	7	8	4	3	3	10
Product (1)	10	4	6	5	6	10
Promotion (4)	6	10	3	2	5	10
Service/support (5)	6	9	4	4	5	10
Sales ('000m²)	1,650	3,015	1,650	2,345	3,685	21,105
Market share (%)	5	9	5	7	11	63
Share trend	up	down	down	same	down	same

Key conclusion: Our performance is relatively good in areas of customer importance but we still need to improve to be superior to competitor F.

5. Supporting strategies to meet marketing objective

Product: Introduce new profiles
Develop larger packs

Price: Position between metal roofing and tiles but 5% less than present

Promotion: Continue builders' program
Develop architects' kit

Distribution: Increase the number of installers

Service/support: Improve the range of fixing tools

6. Expenditure breakup – year 1

Area of expenditure	Amount
Market research	$140K
Point of sale	$150K
Advertising and promotion	$900K
Sales staff training	$220K
Total	**$1,410K**

7. Tactical plan

(Some supporting strategies have been expanded.)

Strategy	Tactics	Results	Timing
Introduce new profiles	Add 3 new profiles	Change sales mix	December Year 1
	Delete 1 old profile	Increase average selling price	December Year 1
	Review accessories	Enhance product	June Year 2
Develop larger packs	Design larger packs	Increase stockists	June Year 1
	Organise customer storage	Lower pack costs	December Year 1

Tactical planning table (cont'd)

Strategy	Tactics	Results	Timing
Price between metal roofing and tiles	Target 15% above metal price for base	Viewed as premium product	June Year 1
	Maintain premium for new profiles	Increase average selling price	December Year 1
Continue builders' program	Direct marketing program	Increase in builder database	January Year 2
	Hit trade media	15% increase in sales	December Year 2
Develop architects' kit	Information packs for architects and specifiers	50% increase in specification of product	December Year 2

Case Study – The Crucible Group

The Crucible Group is an Australian Company formed in 2005 by Joe Herbertson and Les Strezov. They initially were a consulting group but by 2011 they had an invention that they wanted to commercialise.

The Crucible Group has taken its patented Continuous Biomass Conversion technology to the commercialisation stage. The technology features a unique thermo-chemical profile that provides a step change in performance, a flexible feedstock and product platform with opportunities in a wide range of industrial, urban and agricultural sectors and attractive capital pay-back periods for users of the technology.

The technology is global in nature, providing practical and targeted business solutions for industry and agriculture in a sustainable fashion, beyond the realms of solar and wind. It addresses fundamental challenges of climate change, waste, soil quality, energy and food security.

The technology has great promise as customers find specific supply chains that suit them. This case study shows the great resilience that is required in capital intensive inventions.

Below is The Crucible Group story in Joe Herbertson's own words.

———————

The Crucible Group was formed in 2005 as a two-person consultancy promoting sustainability-driven innovation, grounded in technical excellence. Dr Les Strezov and I wanted to draw on the knowledge we had gained over long and successful research careers at BHP to help find fundamental solutions to the challenges of climate change in particular.

We discovered exciting possibilities for substituting fossil fuel derived energy and materials with biomass-based products. But we also quickly discovered that the available biomass processing technologies didn't stack up against the fossil mainstream.

So, without a prior grand plan, we progressively morphed from consulting back to invention, with a team of over ten people primarily ex-BHP Research staff. We soon developed patented ideas for a low-cost, high-productivity algae bio-reactor, a carbon fuel cell for high efficiency, renewable electricity generation and a fundamentally novel approach to biomass pyrolysis. Ultimately, we focused on the latter invention, known as the Continuous Biomass Converter (CBC), taking it from concept to commercialisation. The CBC very effectively converts biomass wastes and residues into three valuable products: a carbon rich char, a clean burning gas and a condensate known as wood vinegar.

Our journey has followed a relatively linear pathway of internal technical development, from modelling, to bench experiments, to an engineering prototype and, for some years now, a commercial scale pilot plant. But the journey has been marked by major shifts in emphasis, driven by external factors (the wider 'innovation ecosystem'), such as funding opportunities and industry collaborations. The market focus of potential early adopters of the technology has been a strong influence on that journey, including:

- Soil improvement from wheat straw-derived char and gas-derived power in regional WA.
- Renewable energy generation by co-firing char at Delta Electricity's Vales Point coal power station.
- Resource recovery of engineered timber wastes currently destined for landfill, in collaboration with Laminex and Newcastle Council's Summerhill Waste Management Centre.
- Value from problematic wastes, such as quarantine flight catering waste, working closely with Qantas.
- Wood vinegar as a high-value product in agriculture, with performance benefits for soils, plants and livestock, working in partnership with market leader Northside Industries.
- Energy sufficiency from CBC processing of macadamia nut shells by Jindilli Farms, with added revenues from char and wood vinegar product sales.

We have demonstrated that the technology has potential across multiple sectors of the manufacturing, agriculture and waste industries.

Funding (around $15 million to date) has been an ever-present challenge for a start-up technology company, coming so far from internally generated funds (30%), industrial collaborators (30%), government grants (15%), R&D tax incentives (15%), and angel investors (10%).

The Hunter Angels (including Eileen), who invest as a group and additionally as individuals, are at this point our only external shareholders. They have been very important to us, not just for funds, but for advice, and for moral support. Like The Crucible Group, they are all from Newcastle and the Lower Hunter. They are highly experienced and successful business people and professionals, who offer wise counsel. Many have engaged with our company in their personal capacities as engineers, lawyers and customers of our products. Glenn Turner and Neville Sawyer, our non-executive directors, have strong business and innovation credentials and have persistently supported the company through its ups and downs, way beyond the call of duty.

Presently we still sit in the often-painful space between invention (better technical solutions) and innovation (market acceptance). It's little wonder this is sometimes called 'crossing the chasm'.

Our overriding priority is the establishment of a commercial reference plant, operating around the clock, proving the process technology and engineering over extended periods, testing the market with significant volumes of products and demonstrating the commerciality of the business. We have been at the cusp for some time, but the first fully commercial project is not yet locked in, although a number of prospects are close to that critical milestone.

We face three interrelated challenges:

1. **Finances:** Ironically, funding is far more difficult to obtain when crossing the chasm than on either side of it (at least, from our experience, in the Australian context). Being largely beyond R&D and not yet ready for the banks, it is a difficult place for the technology company and the early project developer alike.

2. **Business partner:** From our experience, large, successful companies are very often risk averse when it comes to technologies not fully proven. The right business partner at this stage for us is therefore not focused primarily on risk minimisation (although risk management is obviously important), but sees strategic and distinct competitive advantages from being a successful early adopter. Our prospective early adopters have that entrepreneurial approach to innovation.

3. **Regulations:** Government agencies tend to be 'innovation friendly' at the R&D stage. But in our experience, as we moved closer to industrial deployment of the technology, regulators (with compliance in their DNA) are out of their comfort zone with innovation, and more often than not become a source of undue obstacles and time delays. The scope and site of the first commercial reference plant will certainly depend strongly on the approvals pathway.

Ultimately the journey to commercialisation is a major personal challenge for the inventors themselves who come from a research culture. Everyone discovers that things take much longer and require much more money than we ever envisaged. Knowing oneself, learning from mistakes, letting go and finding inner strength are all vital. As a favourite song of mine goes: 'everybody needs an angel, but here's that devil by my side'. Innovation is extremely rewarding and exhausting at the same time. And on this journey, I am personally very grateful for the support of the Hunter Angels at all levels.

Dr Joe Herbertson, AM, 2018, Founder and CEO

CHAPTER 7
THE PORTFOLIO TOOLKIT

Project portfolio plans are useful in clarifying the portfolio of development work that is being undertaken in your organisation to support the business plan and strategic direction.

Key elements of a development plan

The fundamental areas of a development plan are:

► Strategic direction

► Product development/process improvement mix

► Time profile of projects

► Project portfolio mix

► Project list.

Strategic direction

Your company's longer-term strategic direction drives your development plan. It is valuable to clearly state your strategic intent as a lead in to your development plan. This provides an emphasis for your selection of projects.

An example strategic intent statement would be:

To significantly grow our business through the introduction of new product lines and new product groups.

Product development/process improvement mix

Your development plan should reflect the strategic intent of your company. Strategic intent generally fits into the categories of success through a low-cost, efficiency position or success through growing a differentiated product range.

Figure 7.1 gives an overview of the category of development projects given strategic intent and development emphasis. The shaded areas imply the major emphasis for development projects given a low-cost or differentiated strategic intent.

Figure 7.1 – Portfolio product/process mix

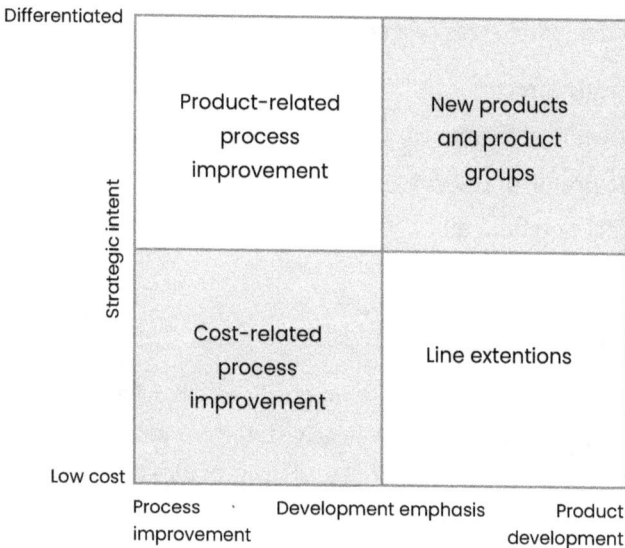

You should plot the mix of your development projects and be comfortable that they align with your company's strategic intent. A typical plot will appear later in the sample plan.

Time profile of project portfolio

To get the best out of your portfolio of projects it needs to be progressively supplying some commercial gain to your business. A valuable way to assess the timeliness of your development work is to group your projects into a time profile histogram. An example is given in Figure 7.2.

Figure 7.2 – Time profile of projects

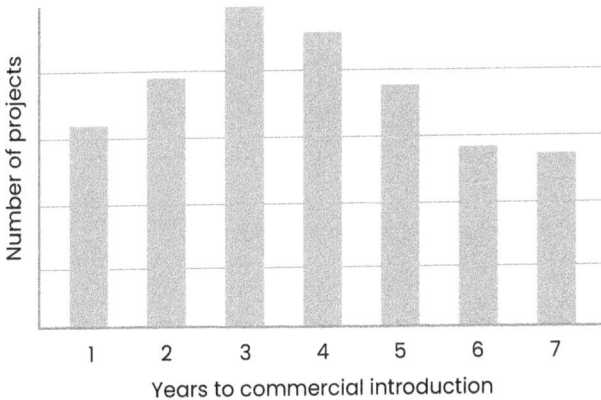

If there is not a reasonable spread in the timeframe for delivery of your projects, your company will experience some competitive time gaps. These need to be addressed by new projects or purchased technology.

Project portfolio mix

Development projects are about a balanced approach to risk and reward. It is important that your mix of projects on average gives you a reasonable chance of return. Of course, risk is related to reward, and you will need to take significant risks to get breakthrough work done. However, your project portfolio mix still should ensure that on average you are getting value for your development project dollar. Figure 7.3 below is an example project portfolio mix graph.

Figure 7.3 – Project portfolio mix

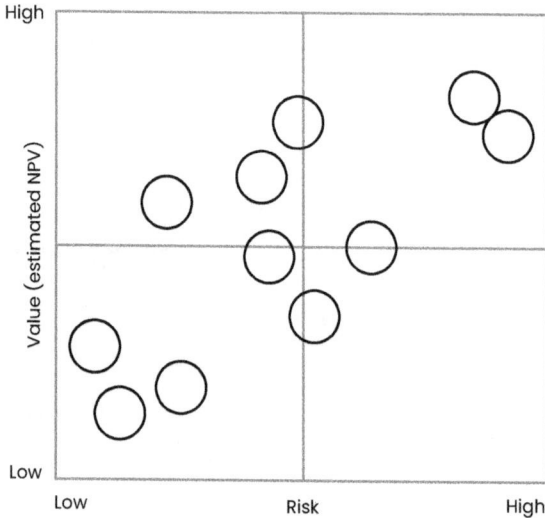

The circles represent the risk/value ratings of individual projects. You need to judge the risk/value mix of projects for your own company in the context of your strategic plan. Obviously, projects that fall in the lower right-hand quadrant of the graph, i.e. low value, high risk, should be avoided.

A full list describing the development projects should back up your plan. The list should at least include details about the project, the timeframe and the project manager. See the example in the sample plan that follows.

Sample development project portfolio plan

To provide an example of a completed basic development project portfolio plan, below I have put together a sample plan for a manufacturing company.

Sample development project portfolio plan

1. Strategic direction

To significantly grow our business through the introduction of new product lines and new product groups.

2. Product/process mix

	Differentiated	
	Product-related process improvement 6	New products and product groups 8
Strategic intent	Cost-related process improvement 7	Line extentions 8
Low cost	Process improvement	Product development
	Development emphasis	

Key conclusion: There is an even mix of our process improvement and our product development. There is also an even mix of our minor and major product development. This spreads our risk and provides a higher chance of success.

3. Time profile of projects

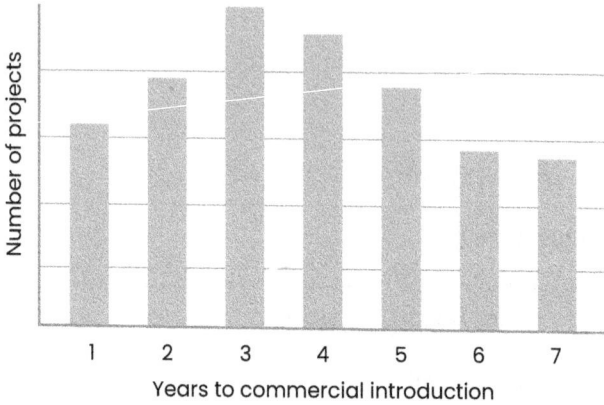

Number of projects (y-axis) vs Years to commercial introduction (x-axis: 1 2 3 4 5 6 7)

Key conclusion: The commercialisation timeframe for our research projects has a healthy distribution over the next seven years. This even spread leads to a sustainable business model

4. Project portfolio mix

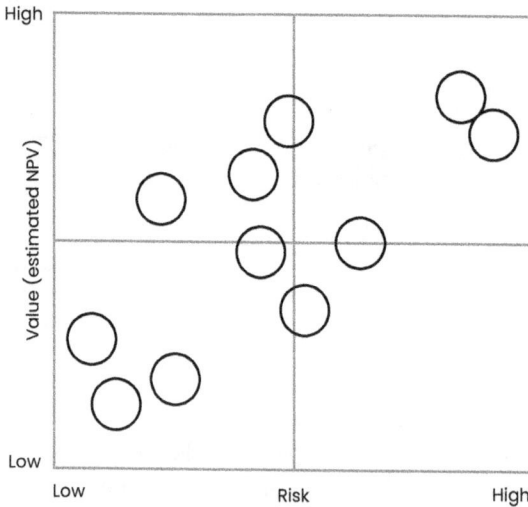

Value (estimated NPV) from Low to High on the vertical axis; Risk from Low to High on the horizontal axis.

Key conclusion: Our higher risk projects have higher rewards. We have some projects with potential high rewards where we have reduced the risk.

5. Project list

Project	Year complete	Manager
1. Enhanced product A	Year 1	BM
2. Product finishing cost reduction	Year 2	AS
3. New product E	Year 2	LF
4. New product F	Year 3	LF
5. Enhanced product B	Year 3	BM
6. More flexible packing line	Year 3	AS
7. Enhanced product C	Year 4	NP
8. New product G	Year 4	BM
9. Improved transport system	Year 4	AS
10. New product H	Year 5	LF
11. Enhanced product D	Year 5	NP
12. New product testing process	Year 6	AS
13. New product I	Year 6	LF
14. New product J	Year 7	BM

CHAPTER 8
THE TRACKING TOOLKIT

Once you have your strategic direction and business plan in place, it is critical to have some simple tracking systems operating. There is no need to swamp yourself with a mass of performance measures. What you need are the few key performance measures that tell you if you are on track with your plan. Gut instinct, conversations with managers and sales staff are no substitute for the facts.

The discipline of regular performance tracking

Your key performance measures should relate to your broad long-term strategies and the 'key measures of success' on your business plan. The discipline of performance tracking is a necessary follow-up to all the good work you have put in place with the long-term and short-term planning for your business.

Performance measures pinpoint your present position and tell you if you need to consider corrective action. If you have the discipline of performance tracking and corrective action, your business will have a far greater chance of being successful.

Measurement timeframes

You will use different performance tracking measures over different timeframes. The relevant timeframe for a measure is determined by a number of factors.

Ease of data collection

The first factor is the ease of collection of the data. The automation of data collection or the establishment of standard processes can allow easy collection of data. I would initially suggest simple manual systems until you decide on your critical data. This will allow you to display your measures over the most appropriate timeframe.

The meaning of the data collected

The second factor is the meaning of the data collected. It is important that data collected over a specific timeframe is meaningful. You need to be sure that you have gone through a full cycle of events before you collect data on a particular item. For example, it might be useless to analyse daily figures on a particular activity if the daily figures vary significantly but the weekly cycle is meaningful.

Ability to take corrective action

The third factor is your ability to take corrective action. The timeliness of data presentation should relate to your ability to view the measure and take the appropriate action to get back on track.

Some typical timeframes for performance measures are:

► Daily (or by shift)
► Monthly (or weekly)
► Quarterly (or half-yearly)
► Annually.

The following sections will give you examples of some relevant measures in the above categories. The measures will not always be appropriate to your business or your plan, but they will give you an idea of how to track particular areas and how to apply the principles to your business.

Daily measures

Daily measures are useful to keep track of the revenue or operations side of your business. Some typical daily measures could be:

- Sales volume or sales dollars
- Delivery performance
- Production volume
- Quality measures
- Process measures
- Productivity measures.

The particular items that you track on a daily basis will depend on the nature of your business and the relevance of that measure to your business plan targets.

Below are some typical daily measures. The first example is a cumulative chart shown in Figure 8.1 and the second is a control chart shown in Figure 8.2. There could be other simple ways you might want to display daily measures.

Cumulative charts

A cumulative chart is very useful if you have a target for the month and you want to track your daily performance in achieving that target or budget figure. A cumulative chart can provide a lot of information in terms of your actual performance, your budget and your latest forecast.

Figure 8.1 shows a cumulative chart for sales. If you are not reaching your targets you have enough timely information to take corrective action. If your business is more complex than a single product, you might have individual product graphs that make up the total sales to help problem-solve why you are not reaching your target. In Figure 8.1 below, your initial actual sales have suggested a forecast for the month that will beat the budget.

Figure 8.1 – Cumulative daily sales example

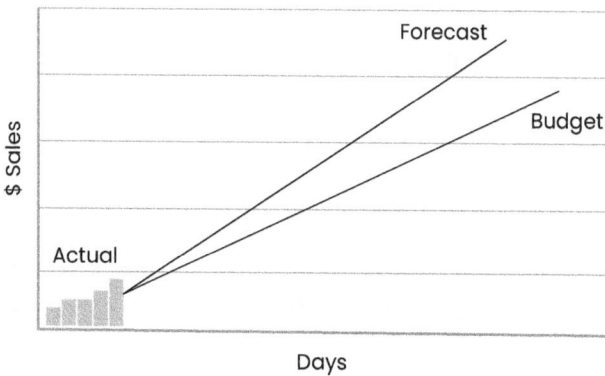

Control charts

Control charting is a major subject in its own right. I will give you a simple example here, but to understand the subject more and before you attempt to control chart anything there are many books you should read on the subject.

In order to plot a control chart, specific data is required. The type of data will determine the type of control chart. Data for quality control work can be divided into two categories:

1. Variables (things you measure)
2. Attributes (things you count as being there or not being there).

Some examples of variables are thickness, diameter, temperature, weight and percentage of impurities.

Some examples of attributes are:

► A product is either defective or not.

► The correct item was either delivered in full on time or not.

► An invoice is complete and correct or not.

Different categories of data require different control charts. To give you an example of a control chart I will concentrate on variable data. This type of data can have an average and range control chart.

Figure 8.2 is an example of a single point moving average control chart, in this case it is measuring the average daily weight of a particular product. This chart indicates that the average daily weight varies around a mean of 5 and is statistically in control around that mean, in the sense that it randomly varies around 5 between the upper and lower control limits (the UCL and LCL).

Figure 8.2 – Average daily product weight control chart example

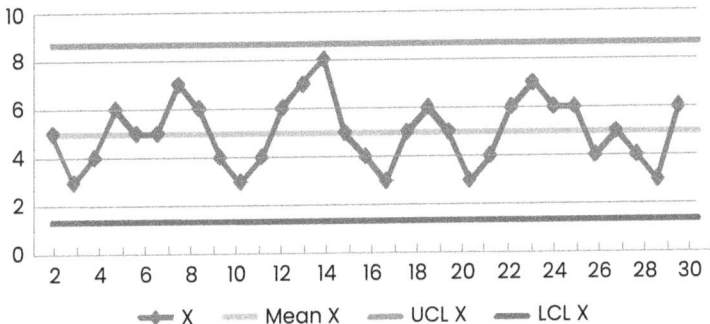

If the customers, for example, require your product to only vary between 3 and 7 then your process is not capable of meeting their needs and you would need to make improvements. Your control chart would then show your product weight having upper and lower control limits between 3 and 7 around a mean of 5. If you need to be below a certain weight for cost purposes, then you can watch for trends (a run of 5 or more) of weight increase and take corrective actions.

Monthly and quarterly measures

Monthly and quarterly measures are useful for keeping track of aspects of your business where you get irregular information or you consolidate the information less frequently. This could be, for example, specific financial information, employee information or customer information.

Figures 8.3 and 8.4 are examples of areas that could be measured on a monthly or quarterly basis.

The first graph is a return tracking chart. It allows you to view your year to date plus forecast performance against the initial budget. It starts with return on capital and then tracks the items that contribute to the return performance. From this sort of chart, you can make the following example statements:

► My EBIT is under budget because the sales are under budget and the energy costs are over budget.

► My working capital is over budget because my raw materials and spares and stores are over budget.

Figure 8.3 – Return tracking example

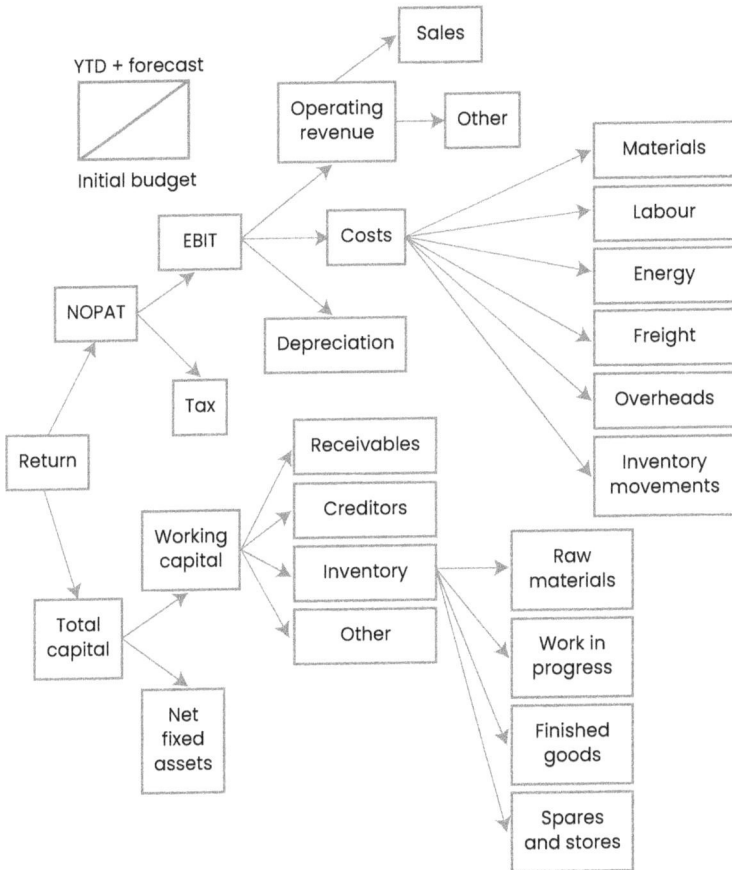

Key:
EBIT – Earnings before interest and tax
NOPAT – Net operating profit after tax

Figure 8.4 gives an example of safety statistics. It shows the actual lost time injury frequency rate for Year 1 and Year 2 and then month by month for Year 3. It also shows the 12-month moving average to give you an indication of the long-term trends.

In this instance, the frequency rate is trending down over time even though there are monthly fluctuations.

Figure 8.4 – Lost time injury frequency rate example

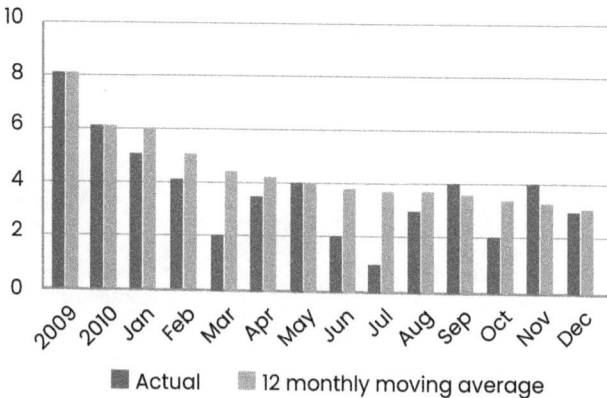

Annual measures

Annual measures are useful for keeping track of aspects of your business where you measure or consolidate the information on an annual basis. This could be, for example, final financial information, employee information, customer information or operations information.

Figure 8.5 gives an example of the possible results from an annual customer survey. As you can see, all areas of customer satisfaction have improved, particularly delivery performance.

Although it takes a long time to collect, annual trend information can be very valuable for future planning and understanding competitive advantage.

**Figure 8.5 – Customer satisfaction example
(Scale 1 to 10)**

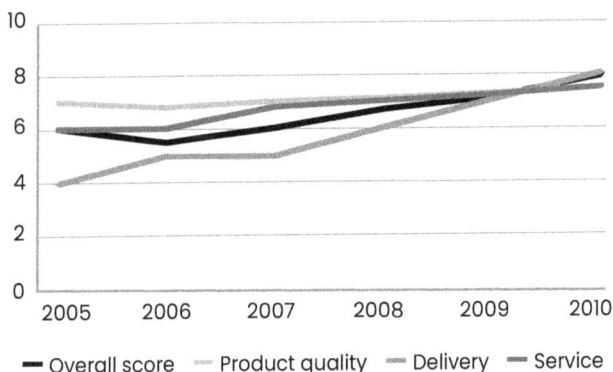

The need to review and correct

Once you have your strategic direction, business plan and performance tracking in place, then the next logical step is to review your performance and take corrective action where necessary.

Your key performance measures should relate to your broad, long-term strategies and the 'key measures of success' on your business plan. The process of review is about ensuring that you are achieving your key measures and the major actions of your business plan.

As I indicated in the previous chapter, the discipline of performance tracking is a necessary follow-up to all the good work you have put in place with the long-term and short-term planning for your business. Performance measures pinpoint your present position and tell you if you need to consider corrective action. It is vital that you put in place a regular review process and take corrective action if you are not achieving your targets.

If you have the discipline of performance tracking and corrective action, your business will have a far greater chance of being successful.

Corrective action from regular performance tracking

The timing of taking corrective action as a result of performance tracking will depend on the measurement timeframes of your performance measures. As indicated in chapter five, the timeliness of data presentation should relate to your ability to view the measure and take the appropriate action to get back on track.

From your regular daily measures, you should be able to view the daily trends and take corrective action over a short timeframe. Your monthly, quarterly and annual measures need to be viewed over their relevant timeframes. Trends in all your performance measures can provide some feedback for your regular business review sessions.

Regular business review sessions

It is good business practice to conduct a regular business review session. The size and complexity of your business will dictate whether this is on a monthly or quarterly basis.

Your business review session should take a look at recent trends in your performance measures and see if any new corrective action plans are required to improve performance.

Your business review session should also review your performance against the action plans you put in place to achieve your business plan. The action plan review example below shows an extra column added onto your original action plan to provide comment for the review. If you were having any major problems keeping on target, then you might add some new corrective action plans.

Action plan review – December Year 1

Action	Timing	Person	Review progress
Broad activity: Process control (PC) measurements			
Develop PC training kit	Aug Year 1	Development manager	Kit in place Pilot group trained
Identify all key factory variables	Jan Year 2	Factory manager	Process mapping complete – all variables listed
Ensure all relevant employees trained	Jan Year 2	Area manager	Training 95% complete
Ensure PC charts in place on factory floor	Jun Year 2	Factory manager	Templates developed

Personal performance reviews

It is good business practice to review your employees' personal performance too. Naturally you should be informally talking about some aspect of performance on a regular basis, but a formal review is an activity you should undertake at least annually.

The personal performance review session should review performance against the personal plans that were put in place for each employee to achieve your business plan. The personal plan review example below shows an extra column added onto your original plan to provide comment for the review. This document provides a good basis for clear formal communication.

Personal plan review – July Year 2

Name: Damien Smith
Period of Plan: Year ended June Year 2

Goals (What and by when?)	Key steps (How will you go about it?)	Measures (How will you know goals were achieved?)	Outcomes (What did you achieve and when?)
Job improvement goals			
Ensure process control measures are in place in cutting and packing area by June 2004	Identify all key factory variables	Variables identified by December Year 1	All variables identified
	Provide training to employees on PC charts	PC charts in place by Jun Year 1	Charts in place and well received by all employees
	Put PC charts on factory floor		**Great job**
Review all standard operating procedures (SPOs) in the cutting and packing area by June 2004	Conduct audit of SOPs to identify problem areas	All SOPs reviewed by January 2004	All SOPs reviewed but still a quality problem in cutting area
	Set up teams to review each SOP in line with audit results		

CHAPTER 9
MAKING IT HAPPEN

The old adage of 10% inspiration and 90% perspiration is clearly valid on your path to commercialising your idea. From a business angel perspective, I would rather have a good idea with a solid set of resources, drive and infrastructure than a great idea with not enough execution support. Once you have refined your idea, most of your effort needs to go into planning the details and working out the resources needed for its commercial execution.

Know yourself

All of us, including entrepreneurs, are not as good as we should be at understanding our strengths and where we add value and the areas where we really need help from others. One thing is clear, the originator of an invention will not have all the skills to develop a commercial innovation.

It is really important that you understand the areas where you can personally add the greatest value and the areas where you need to partner with others to get full value. It is hard for the inventor to let go, but at a point on your path to commercialisation, you will have to. You therefore must know yourself and when it is time to let others in.

One common attribute I have noticed with successful entrepreneurs is resilience. There are continual setbacks to overcome on this path and you must have an underlying resilience to not dwell on the setbacks but to relentlessly find the path forward.

Know your ecosystem

The description of the innovation ecosystem in chapter one gives a generic overview of the important players in the system. Before you try to take advantage of your ecosystem you need to understand it. Whether your ecosystem is based on a physical area or an industry category or a technology platform, you need to get a feel for the contributors.

Given you are the idea generator you need to gain knowledge about the capital funding, the support infrastructure, the talent pool and the potential exit strategies. Your knowledge of this will help you seek out the right players to assist you. You can gain this knowledge by research, attending founders' forums and innovation workshops and just talking to people.

Find the right business angel

There is a variety of angel groups. Some of them stick to a particular industry or technology platform, others are more diverse. Some like to support a particular regional area while others have links with specific universities or venture capital groups, IP advisers or some other part of the innovation ecosystem. It is worth studying the angel groups that are relevant to your idea and making sure you are engaging with those most likely to be attracted to your idea.

Use the toolkits

The concept for this book has been to take the disciplined approach of larger public businesses and my experience as a business angel to help you commercialise your ideas.

My knowledge and experience has been gained over 30 years as a business angel and Top 100 Australian board director. I've also developed some useful toolkits for innovators and start-ups to use in their business journey, which I've included in the book to help you too.

I know you will have some great conversations with your team and you need to. By working through this book and the toolkits you will have a clear pathway to define and explain your idea to others, to determine the future direction and to create a sustainable business.

As I said in the introduction, this book has been created to support the great innovation and free thinking that exists in small, growing companies. It shares knowledge and insights that can support inventors and start-ups and create commercial success.

Many entrepreneurs and small businesses fail not because of a poor idea but because of poor analysis and execution.

Learn from your mistakes

The road to commercialising a new way of doing things is never easy. Nobody takes all the right steps on this path. It takes great resilience to reach established commercialisation and it is not for the faint-hearted. It can create both personal and financial stress. Sometimes you need to stop and regroup and realise your original idea is not viable. Take the lessons from this experience and move onto the next or modified idea.

Failures are an important part of this and are necessary to learn the lessons you need to finally reach your goal. It is important to fail fast and learn from your mistakes. This learning will take you through life and help each time you introduce a new idea. Don't be disheartened. Treat these setbacks as ways to eventually end up with an innovation to be proud of.

Know your exit strategy

From the investors' perspective they only get a financial return on their investment when they are successfully exited. You would have presented some potential exit strategies in your pitch, but opportunities can change over time. It is very important that you regularly review your supply chain (suppliers and customers) and your competitors to look at potential alliances or opportunities for them to buy some or all of your business.

Developing size and scale leads to much improved chances of an exit. This size and scale can also lead to an opportunity for floating your company or bringing in other investors to buy out your original investors. Your original investors need to know that you are actively considering an exit strategy for them and fostering relationships that improve the probability of this happening.

Embrace your journey

Taking an idea or invention on the journey to innovation or sustainable commerciality is like riding on an emotional roller coaster. You can experience the depths of frustration and despair, right up to the heights of satisfaction and celebration and at all the places in between. The key is to have resilience, maintain a positive attitude and rely on clear analysis and data to solve a problem and define a path forward.

Most inventions never make it to innovation but that doesn't mean that the effort is wasted. They build on our knowledge and experience and can also be a starting point for a successful innovation.

Your journey to innovation, along with others on the same journey, is what creates the future and gives hope for a sustainable world.

Embrace your journey.

LIST OF ABBREVIATIONS AND GLOSSARY OF TERMS

Book value – value of a security or asset as entered in a company's books

CBC – continuous biomass converter

Drag along rights – forced to take same price and terms as majority shareholders

EBIT – earnings before interest and tax

GDP – gross domestic product

Investor control rights – listed rights of investors

MVP – minimum viable product

NPV – net present value

NOPAT – net operating profit after tax

OH&S – occupational health and safety

Pre-emptive rights – right to maintain ownership percentage through purchase

R&D – research and development

ROFE – return on funds employed

SOPs – standard operating procedures

Subscription share rights – non dilutive way to raise capital

SWOT – strengths, weaknesses, opportunities and threats

Tag along rights – forces majority shareholder to join minority shareholders in a transaction at same terms

WACC – weighted average cost of capital

INDEX

www.ingramcontent.com/pod-product-compliance
Lightning Source LLC
Chambersburg PA
CBHW031936190326
41519CB00007B/552